The Art of the Goldsmith in
Late Fifteenth-Century Germany

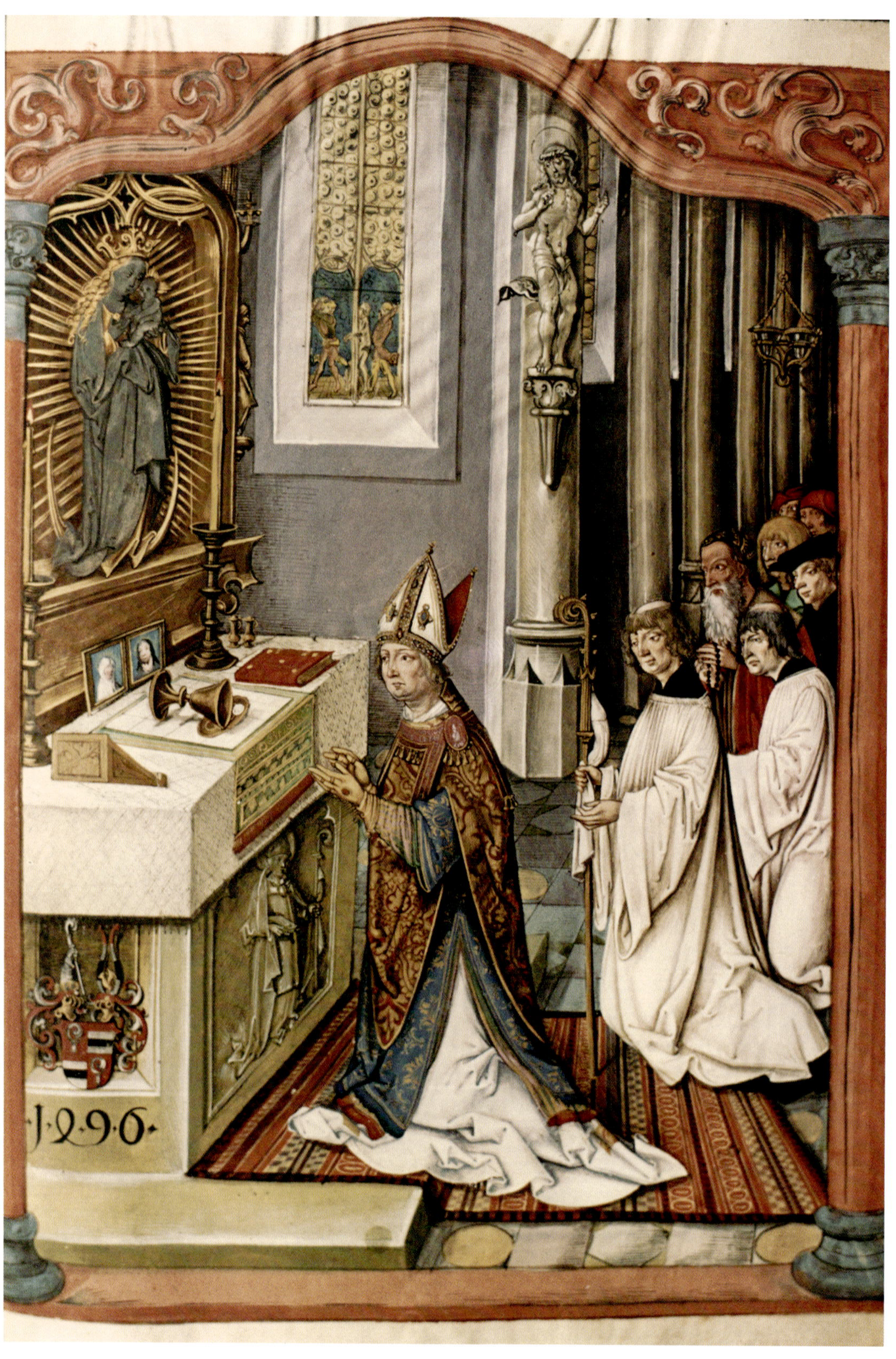
1496

The Art of the Goldsmith in Late Fifteenth-Century Germany

The Kimbell Virgin and Her Bishop

JEFFREY CHIPPS SMITH

Kimbell Art Museum

Fort Worth

DISTRIBUTED BY

Yale University Press

New Haven and London

KIMBELL MASTERPIECE SERIES

Published by Kimbell Art Museum, Fort Worth
Distributed by Yale University Press, New Haven and
London

© 2006 by Kimbell Art Museum
3333 Camp Bowie Boulevard
Fort Worth, Texas 76107-2792
www.kimbellart.org

Yale University Press
302 Temple Street
P.O. Box 209040
New Haven, Connecticut 06520-9040
www.yalebooks.com

Produced by the publications department of the
    Kimbell Art Museum.
Wendy P. Gottlieb, Manager of Publications
Lindsay E. Askins, Publications Assistant
Tom Dawson, Museum Designer
Robert LaPrelle, Kimbell Art Museum photography

Printed in Singapore by CS Graphics

LIBRARY OF CONGRESS CATALOGING-IN-PUBLICATION DATA
Smith, Jeffrey Chipps, 1951-
    The art of the goldsmith in late fifteenth-century
Germany : the Kimbell Virgin and her bishop / Jeffrey
Chipps Smith.
        p. cm.—(Kimbell masterpiece series)
    Includes bibliographical references.
    ISBN-13: 978-0-912804-45-3
    ISBN-10: 0-912804-45-9 (Kimbell pbk. : alk. paper)
    ISBN-13: 978-0-300-11736-3
    ISBN-10: 0-300-11736-1 (Yale pbk. : alk. paper)
    1. Virgin and Child (Silver figurine) 2. Silverwork—
Germany, Southern—History—15th century. 3. Wilhelm,
von Reichenau, Bishop of Eichstätt, ca. 1426-1496—Art
patronage. 4. Silverwork—Texas—Fort Worth. 5.
Kimbell Art Museum. I. Title.
    NK7150.A3S68 2006
    739.2'3094309024—DC22
                                        2006013727

Cover illustrations: Details of the *Kimbell Virgin and Child*,
1486. Silver, parcel-gilt, stones (opal, clear and pale sapphires,
garnets, and pale emeralds), height 20⅞ in. (53 cm). Kimbell
Art Museum, Fort Worth

Frontispiece: Augsburg Illuminator, *Wilhelm von Reichenau at
Mass*, from the *Pontifikale Gundekarianum*, c. 1501–2 (fig. 64)

Page vi: Michael Wolgemut and Wilhelm Pleydenwurff,
View of Eichstätt, from Hartmann Schedel's *Liber Chronicarum
[Nuremberg Chronicle]*, Anton Koberger, 1493 (detail of fig. 25)

Contents

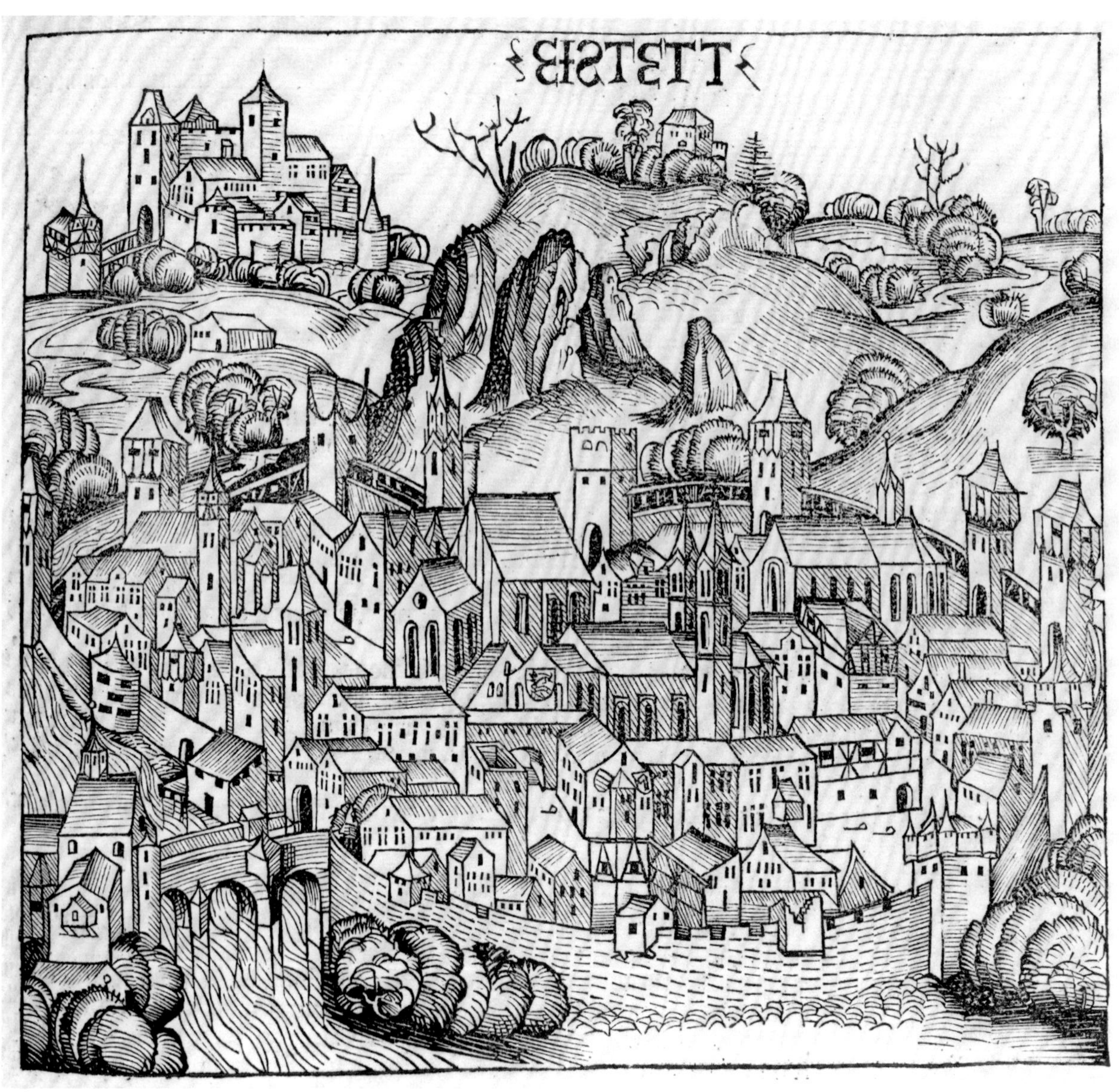
EISTETT

Foreword

The Kimbell's first director, Richard F. Brown, set down the principles upon which the Museum's collection would be founded in his Policy Statement of June 1, 1966:

> The dominating principle involved in the acquisition process is that the stature of the Museum depends more upon the quality of the definitive objects it contains than on the historical completeness of its collections. A prospective addition to the collections, therefore, is to be judged from the standpoint of aesthetic quality and typicality, and whether it defines a master, period, school, style or area. The goal shall be definitive excellence, not size of collection.

The idea that a single great work of art can be "definitive" is the basis for the Kimbell Masterpiece Series, which we launch with Jeffrey Chipps Smith's rich and insightful study of our south German *Virgin and Child*. We have invited leading authorities to discuss individual works from the collection at some length, moving beyond the immediate fact of their great beauty to tease out some of the ways in which they define the cultures that created them.

In selecting works for the series we have favored those that lend themselves to fresh scholarship and connoisseurship. In some cases, including the present one, they are recent acquisitions that were relatively inaccessible, even to specialists, until entering the Museum. In others they are works owned by the Museum for some time about which new information and interpretations have emerged. The next two volumes in the series are in this latter category: the Museum's Senior Curator, Malcolm Warner, will write on Frederic Leighton's portrait of May Sartoris, and Laurence Kanter, Curator-in-Charge of the Robert Lehman Collection at the Metropolitan Museum of Art, New York, will write on Fra Angelico's altarpiece panel *The Apostle Saint James the Greater Freeing the Magician Hermogenes*.

The Kimbell has published many exhibition catalogues but few writings devoted to the permanent collection. We are launching the Masterpiece Series to help fill the gap, providing monographic studies of the highest scholarly caliber that are both valuable to specialists and interesting to the intelligent reader who is not a professional art historian. As the present volume demonstrates, these aims are not incompatible.

Timothy Potts
Director, Kimbell Art Museum

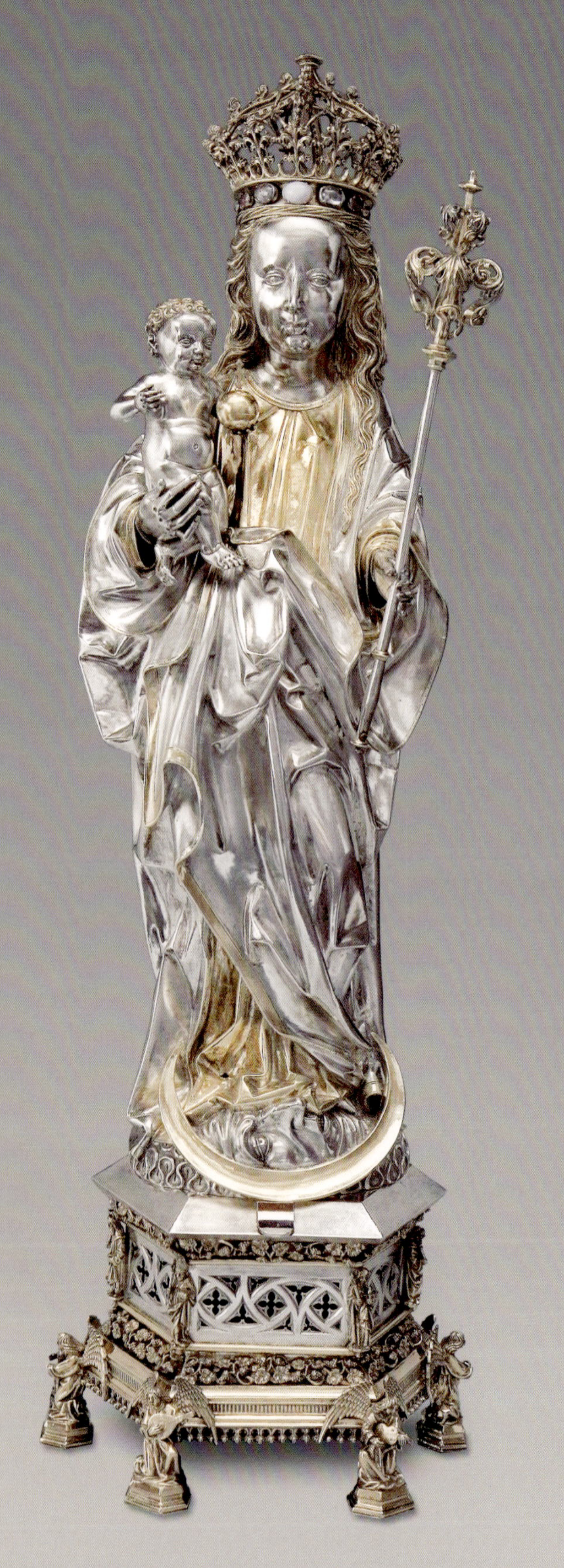

The Statuette: An Introduction

Imaginem argenteam beate Marie Virginis fieri fecit,
et ecclesie cathedrali donauit.
(He [Wilhelm von Reichenau] caused a silver image of
the Blessed Virgin Mary to be made and gave it to the
cathedral church.)

—*Pontifikale Gundekarianum* [1]

On September 6, 2002, the Kimbell Art Museum proudly announced its acquisition of an exquisite silver *Virgin and Child* statuette (fig. 1).[2] Made in south Germany during the late fifteenth century for a powerful bishop, Wilhelm von Reichenau of Eichstätt (r. 1464–96; see figs. 56, 64), this is one of the rare surviving masterpieces of the art of the goldsmith. First recorded in the catalogue of the collection of Mayer Carl von Rothschild in Frankfurt in 1885, the statuette was largely unknown until its sale and inclusion immediately thereafter in the Ulmer Museum's fine exhibition *Michel Erhart & Jörg Syrlin*, in the fall of 2002.[3] The reappearance of such a high-quality object immediately raises questions about its creation, patronage, functions, and relation to other contemporary works. The *Virgin and Child's* very existence, however, is a sobering reminder of how few goldsmith objects from this period survive. This short monograph is an exercise in historical discovery and, I hope for the reader, aesthetic appreciation.

Figure 1. *The Kimbell Virgin and Child*, 1486. Silver, parcel-gilt, stones (opal, clear and pale sapphires, garnets, and pale emeralds), height 20⅞ in. (53 cm). Kimbell Art Museum, Fort Worth

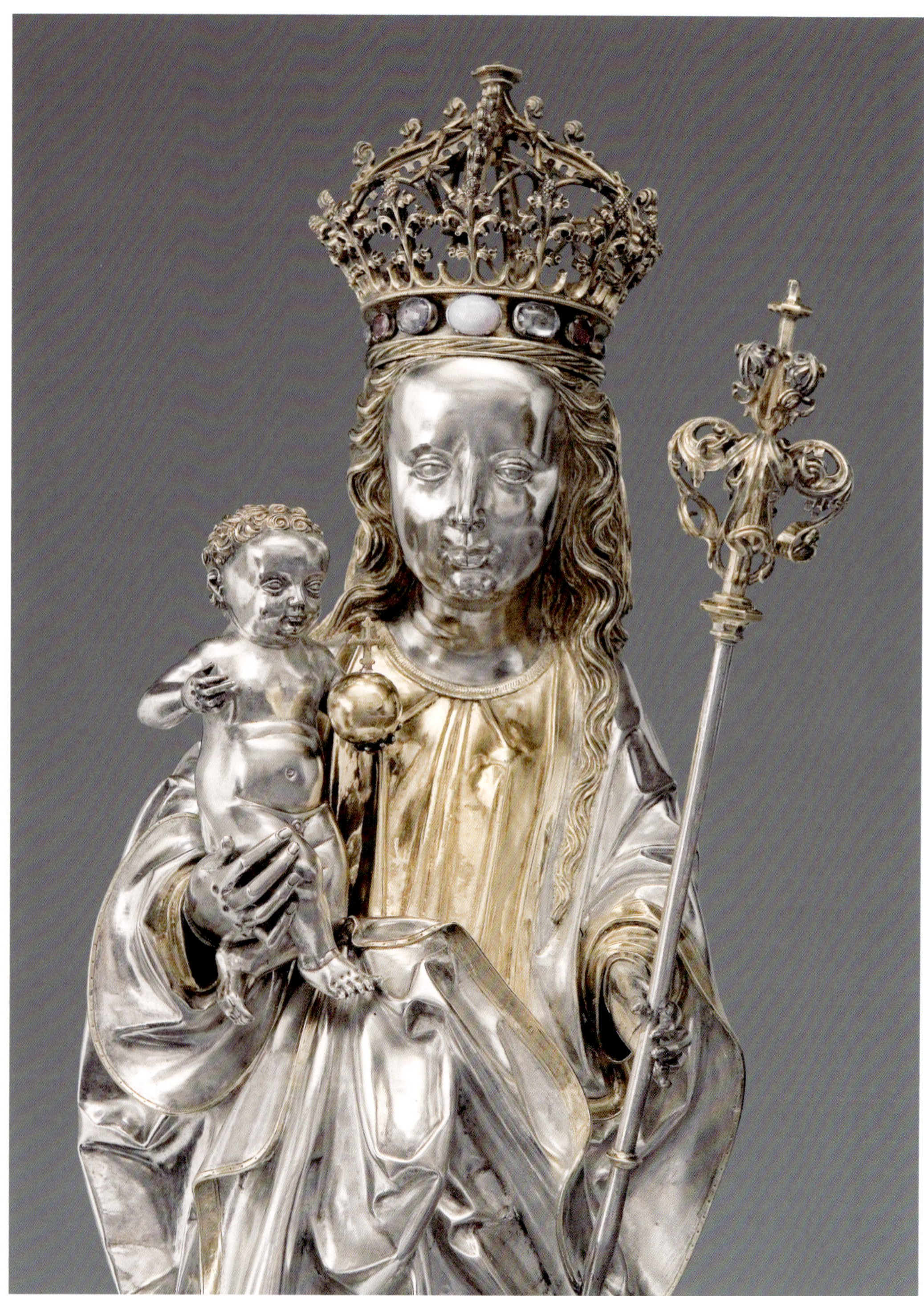

Figure 2. Front of statuette, upper half

The *Kimbell Virgin and Child*, as it will be referred to, stands 20⅞ inches (53 centimeters) high (figs. 2, 3). It is silver with parcel-gilt (partially gold surface) and is largely hollow. (In some photographs, areas that are silver appear to be gilded because of reflections from the gold.) The statuette shows the Virgin of the Apocalypse or the Virgin in the Sun (*Maria in Sole*), a subject that enjoyed great popularity in the fifteenth and early sixteenth centuries (see figs. 16, 26, 37, 51, 69). Revelation 12:1, 5 reads, "And there appeared a great wonder in heaven; a woman clothed with the sun, and the moon under her feet, and upon her head a crown of twelve stars. . . . And she brought forth a man-child, who was to rule all nations." The Virgin is celebrated as mother of Christ and Queen of Heaven. Mary's crown (fig. 4) is ornamented with twelve semiprecious stones, including a creamy opal in the center,

Figure 3. Virgin's head with crown

Figure 4. Crown

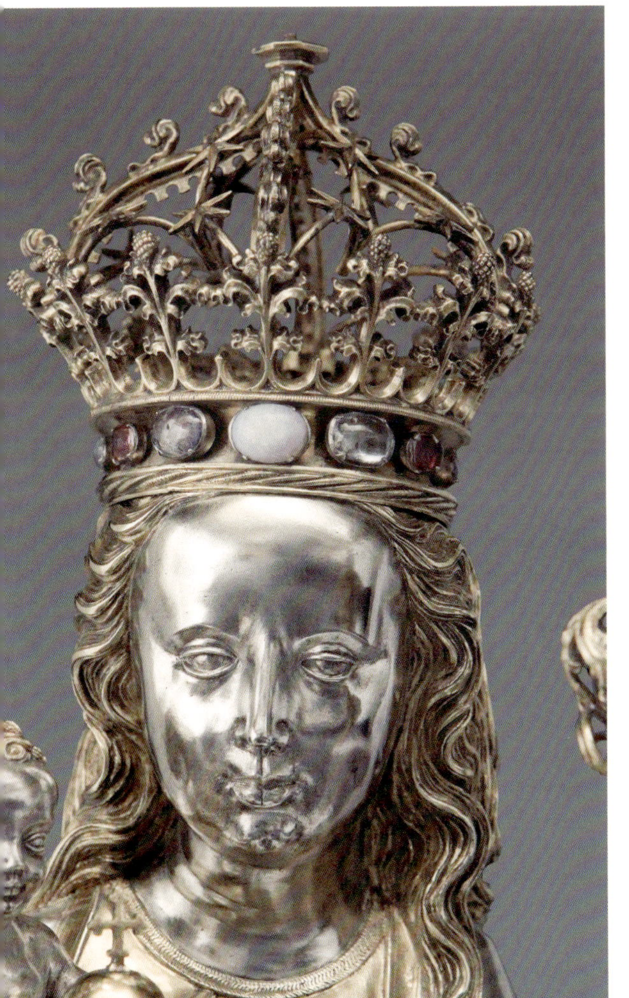

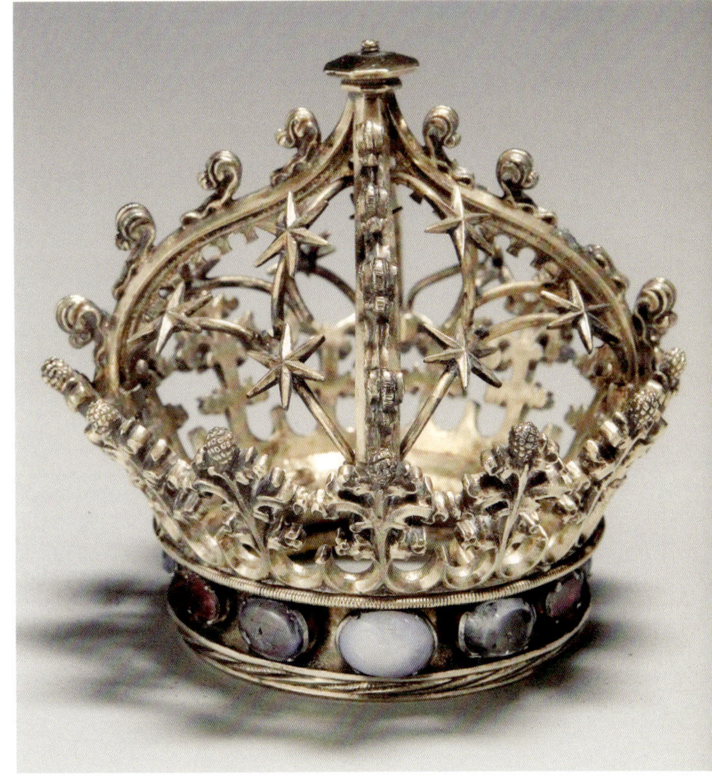

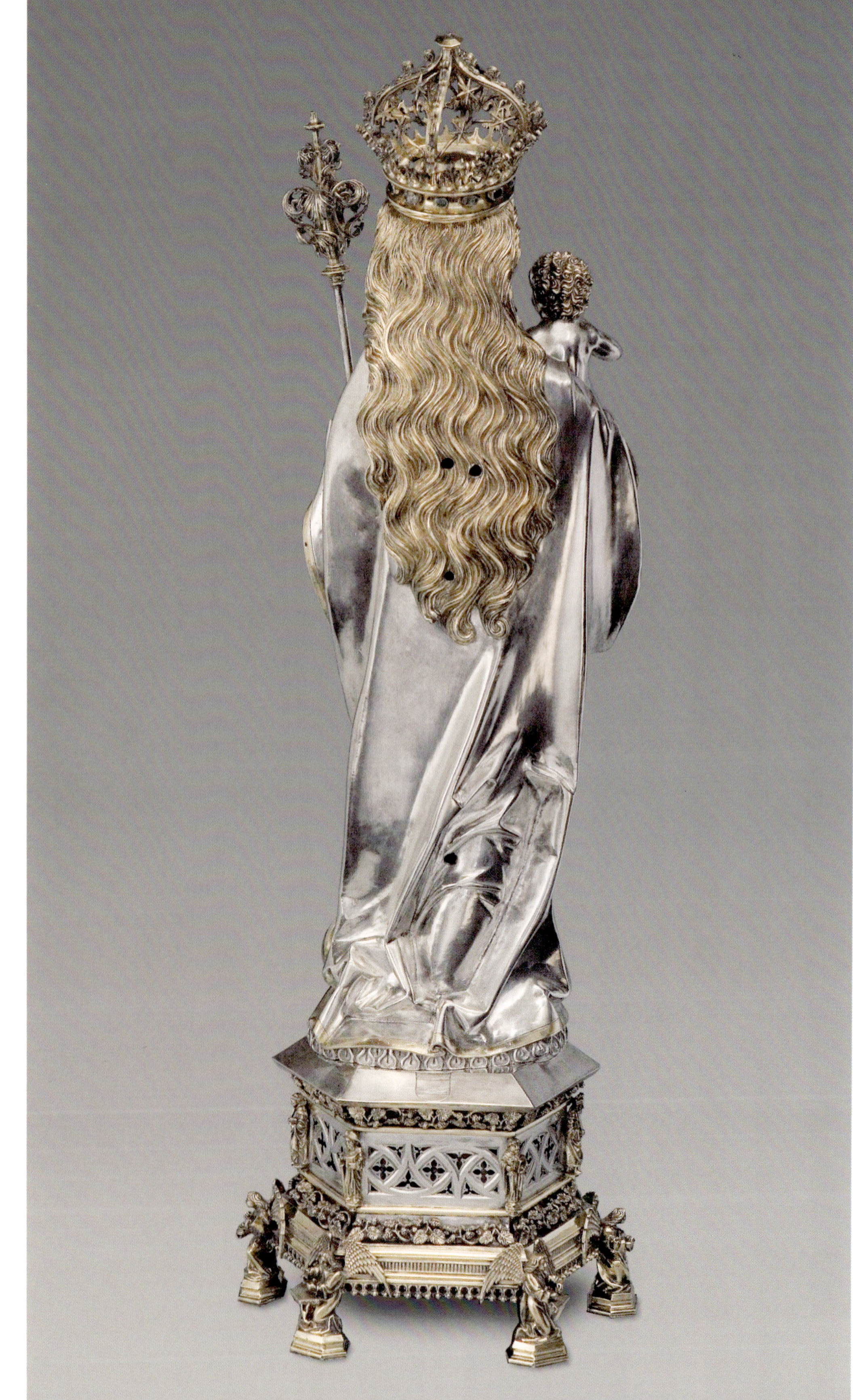

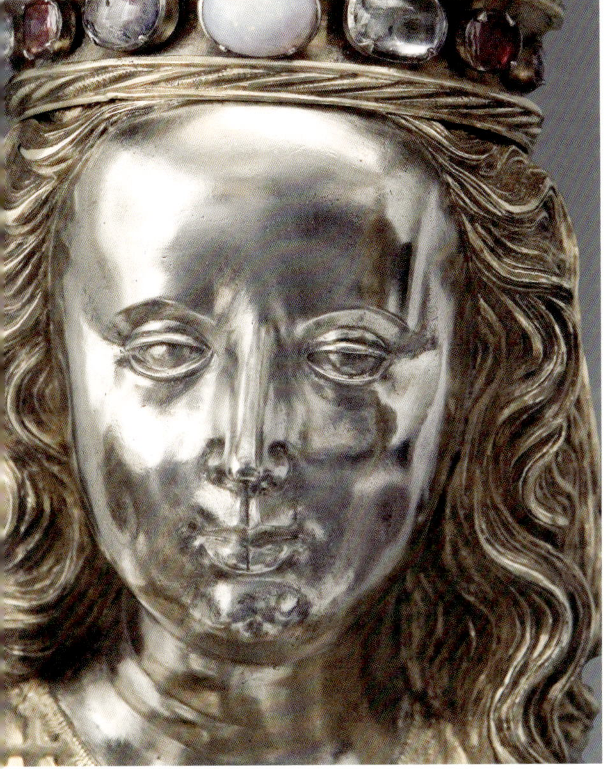

Figure 6. Virgin's face

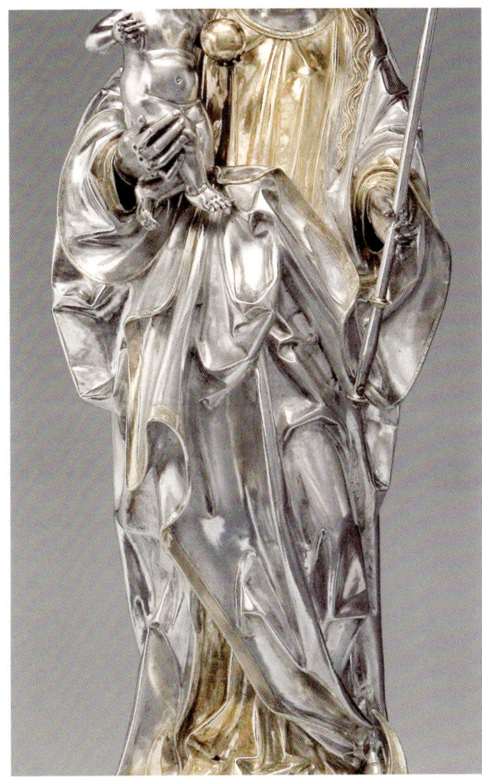

Figure 7. Front drapery

clear and pale sapphires, garnets, and pale emeralds, plus a dozen golden stars. Twelve fleurs-de-lis, an allusion to Mary's royalty, adorn the sides of the crown, whose foliate top, still visible in an 1885 photograph (see fig. 74), subsequently was broken off and lost. Mary's long hair flows luxuriantly over her shoulders and, in back, reaches almost to her waist (fig. 5). One strand trails decoratively over her left shoulder. At some later date, the statuette was outfitted with an aureole of sun rays, now lost, attached by four screws drilled into the back of Mary's hair and robe.

The artist devoted great care to the youthful Virgin's delicate features (fig. 6) and ample robes (fig. 7). Mary's face is a long, relatively thin oval highlighted by a broad forehead, narrow nose, and

Figure 5. View of the back

dimples in her chin and cheeks. She wears a voluminous cloak over a golden dress. As the material gathers at her waist, the drapery forms a rich pattern of angular folds sweeping across the lower half of her body. This attention to surface, accented further by the intricate calligraphy of gilt and punch-ornamented trim of the cloak, animates the statuette. The artist calculated the dynamic effect of light flickering over the statuette's varied surfaces. From behind, the slight movement of Mary's right leg agitates the otherwise smooth lines of the cloak (figs. 8, 9).

Figure 8. Lower half of Virgin, back

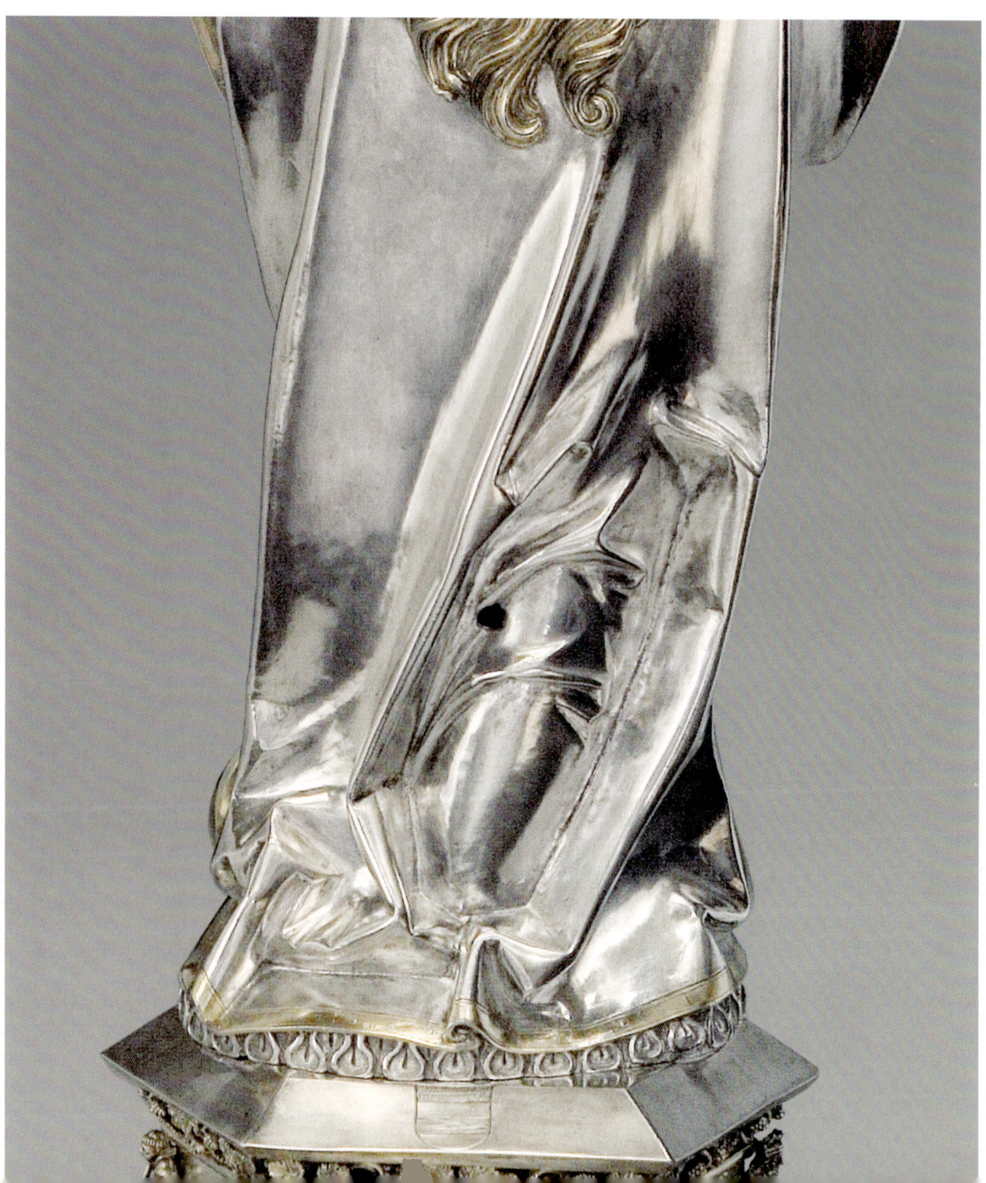

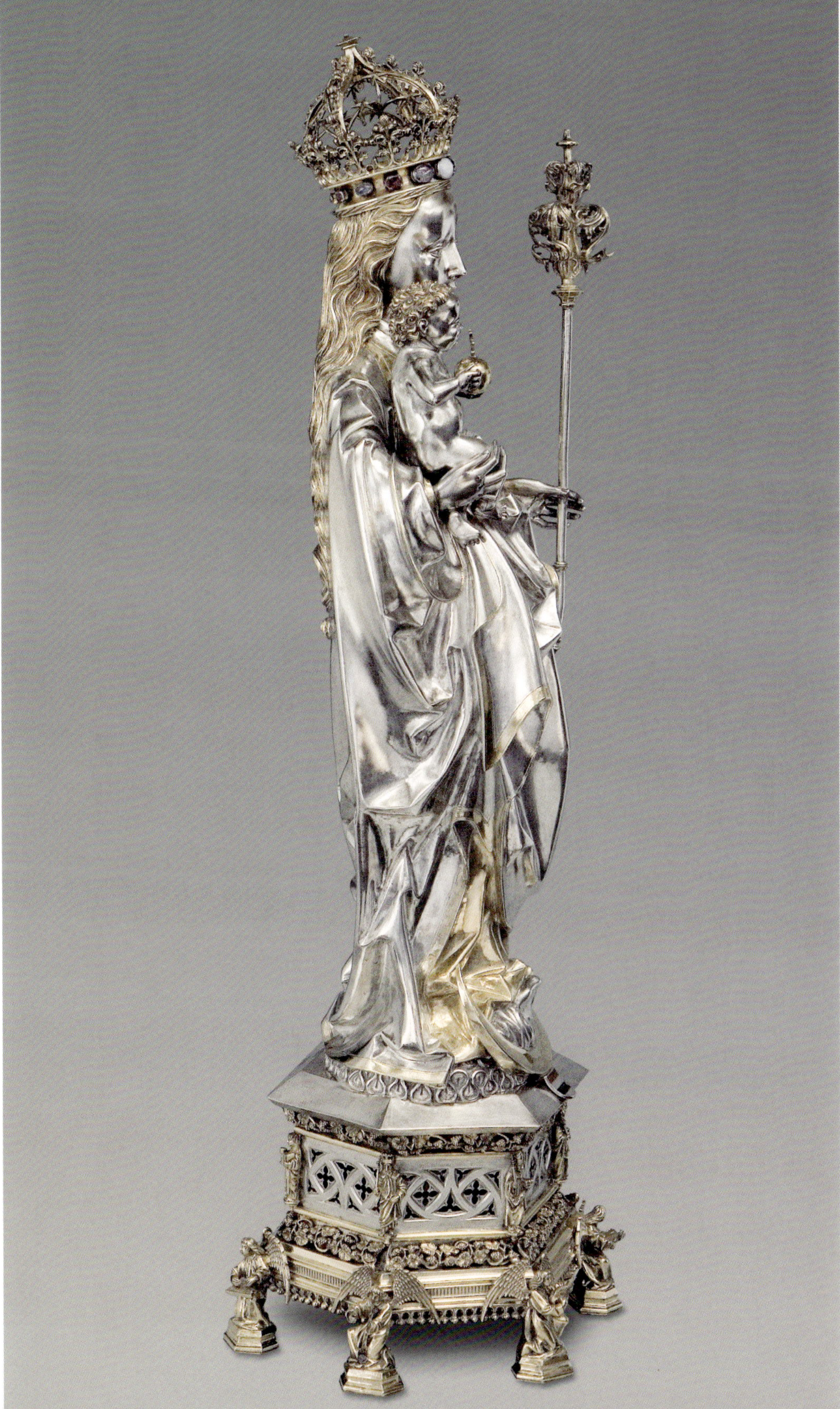

Figure 9.
View of the
left side

The Virgin carries the Christ Child (figs. 10, 11) and, in her left hand, a flowering scepter (see fig. 45), signifying her celestial authority. Mary securely supports her son, her fingers pressing gently into his right thigh. The pudgy stomach, soft flesh, and dimples are realistically a child's (fig. 12). The artist's virtuosity is evident in the pose of the legs, especially how the left crosses beneath the right and lightly touches Mary's hand. Christ holds the world orb, a common symbol of his earthly and heavenly reign. It is uncertain whether the cross on the top of the orb is the original or a later addition or replacement.

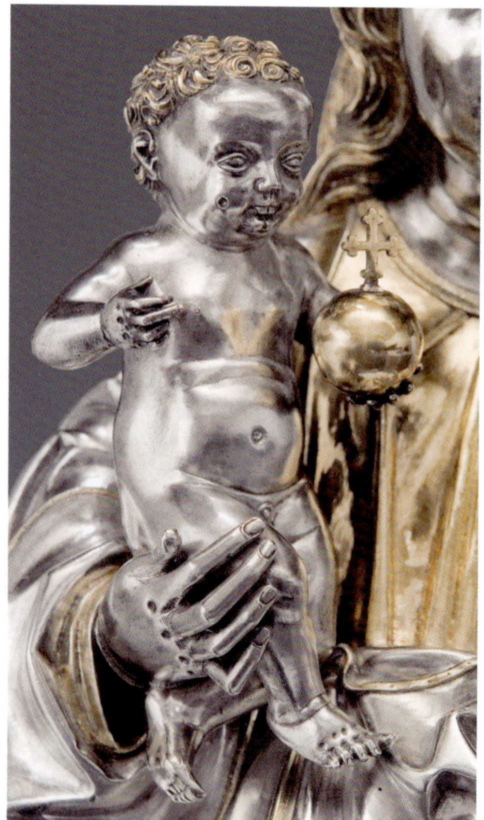

Figure 10. Christ Child

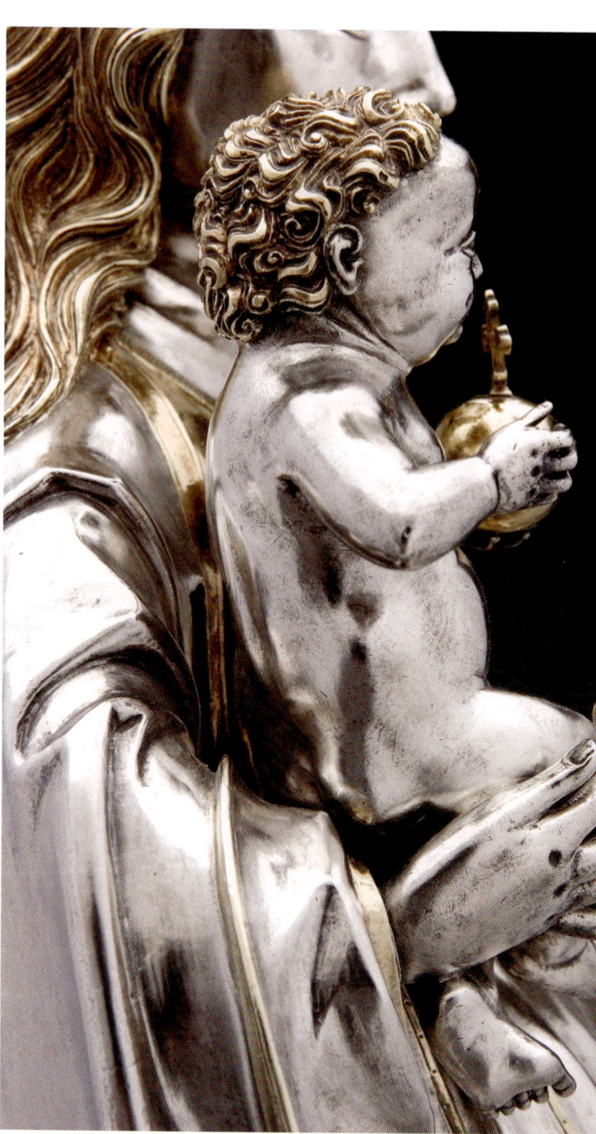

Figure 11. Christ's and Virgin's right hands

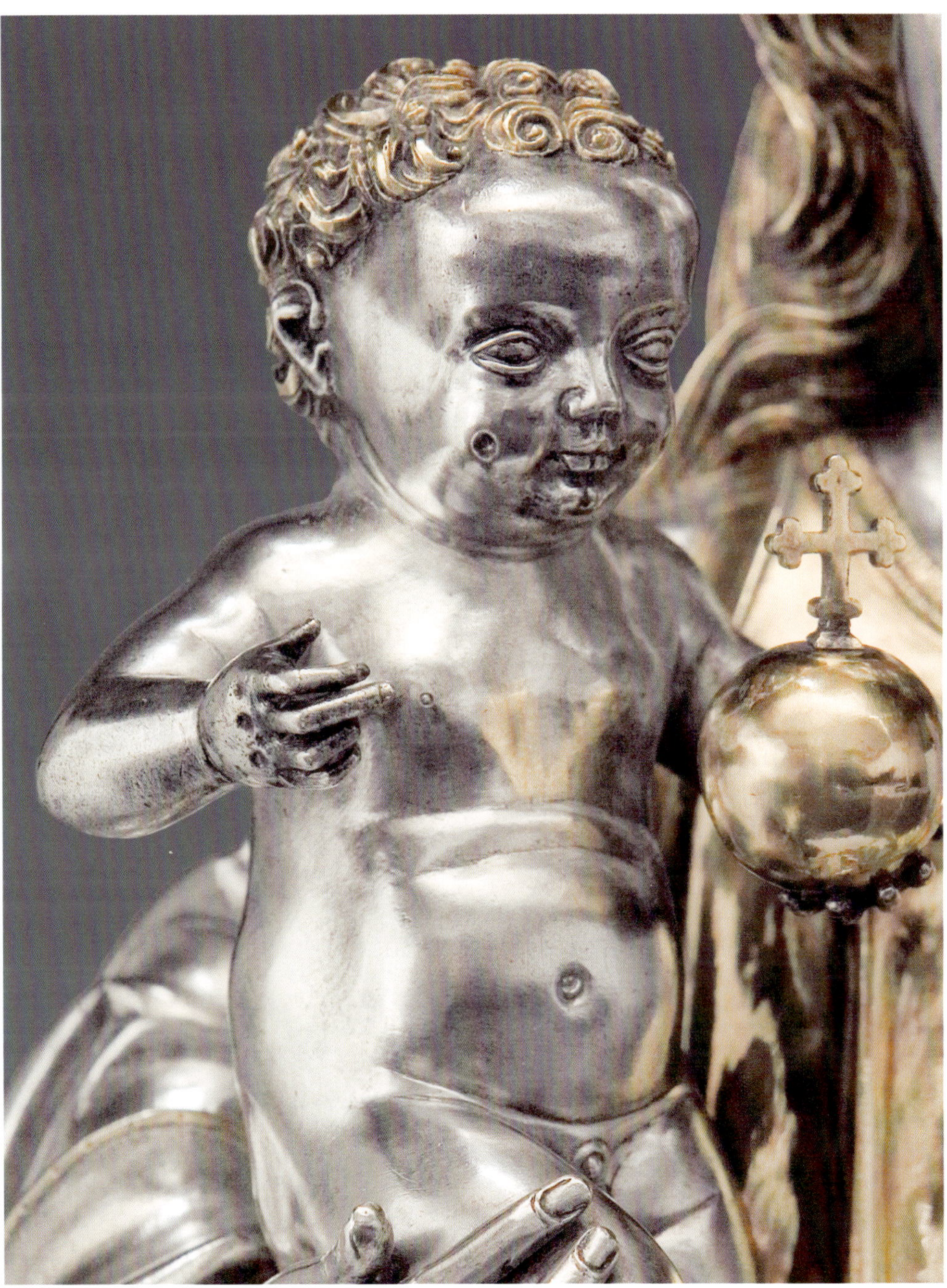

Figure 12. Christ's shoulders and head

Figure 13. Plinth and base

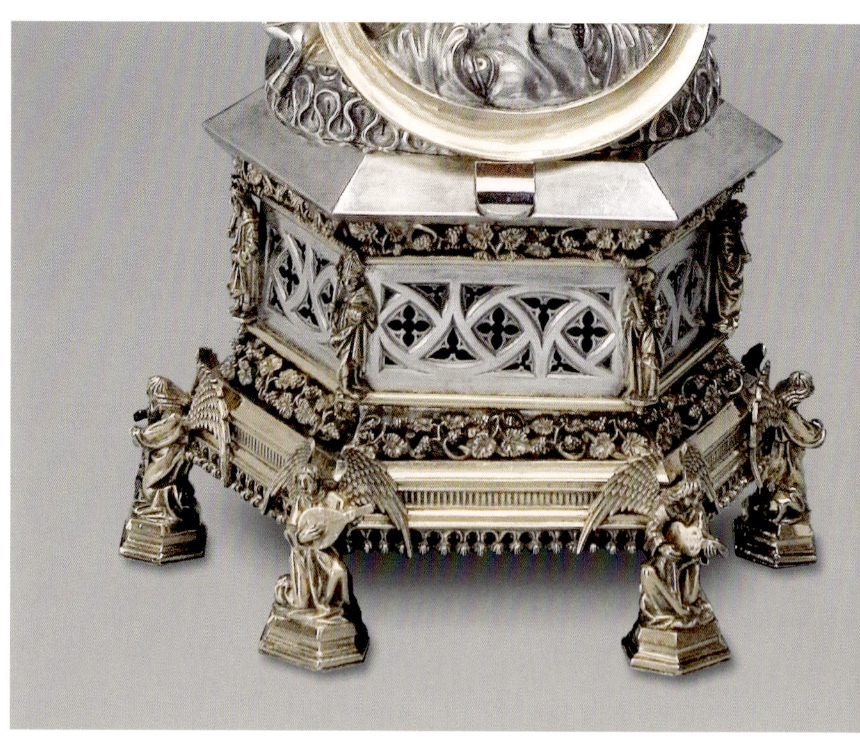

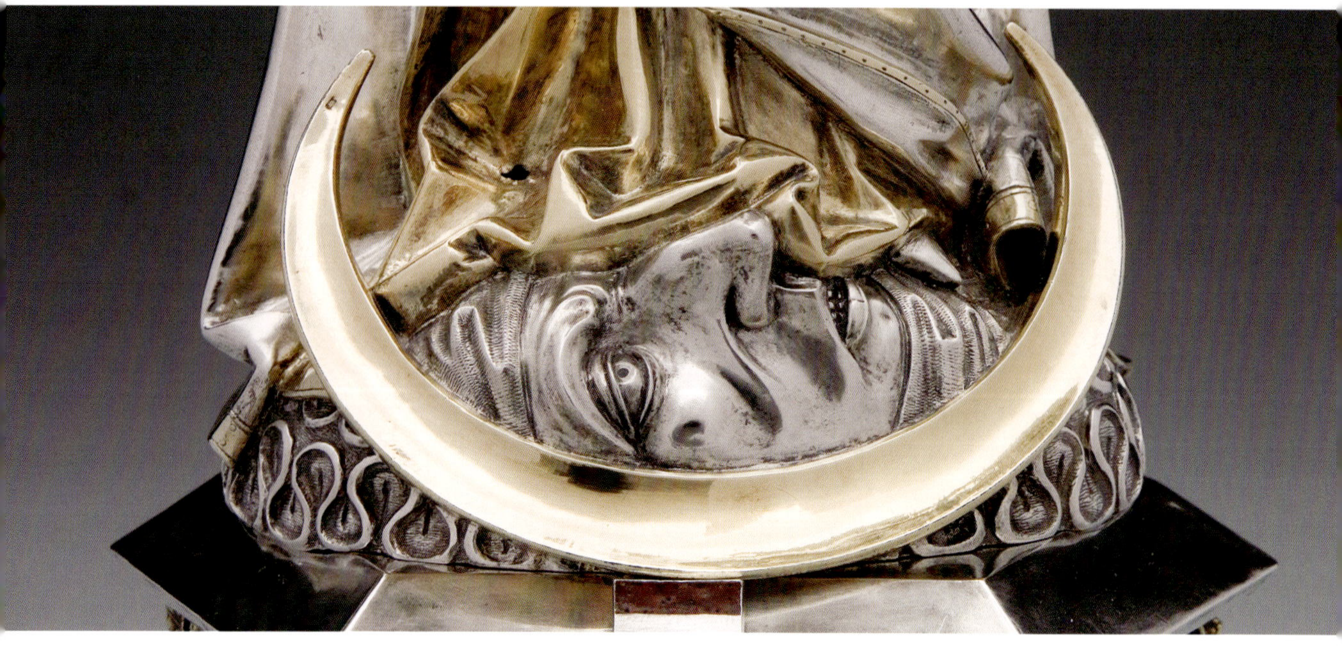

Figure 14. Crescent moon and clouds

Mary stands upon a crescent moon set on a hexagonal silver plinth surmounting a base (figs. 13, 14, 15). As was common, the moon is personified as a human face in profile. Beneath floats a bank of stylized, scallop-shaped clouds, signifying the Virgin's timeless placement above the heavens. Note how the artist skillfully alternated the two colors of his materials. The silver clouds are followed by the gilt crescent, the silver face, the gilt hem of Mary's dress, the silver cloak, and so on up to the apex of her crown. Only the red, silver, black, and silver bands of Bishop Wilhelm's arms on the shield beneath the crescent moon slightly disturb this rhythm.

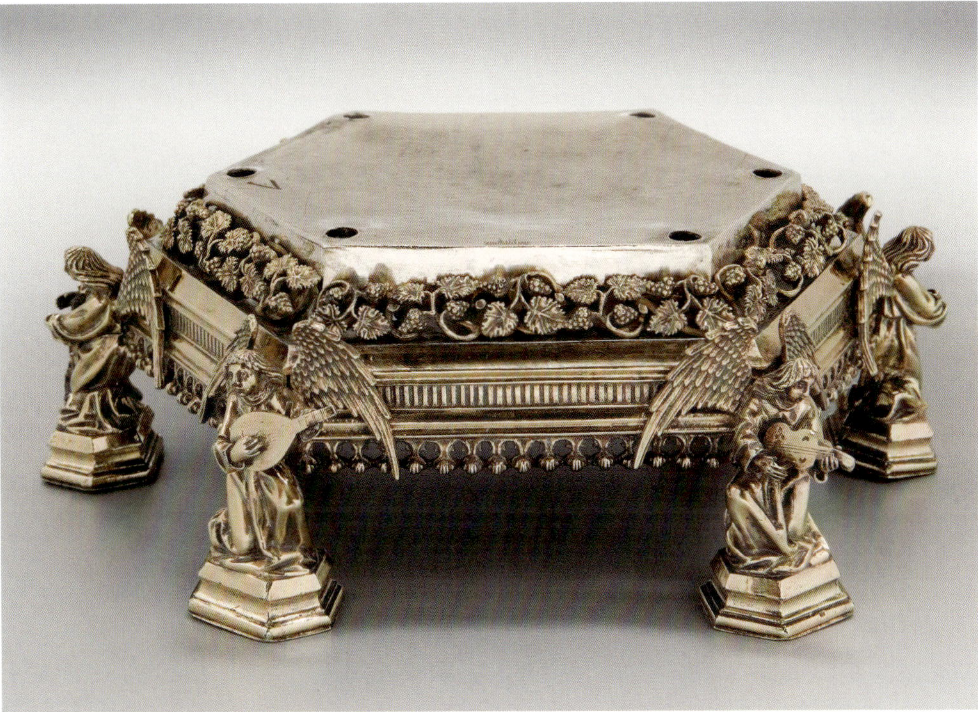

Figure 15. Lower half of base

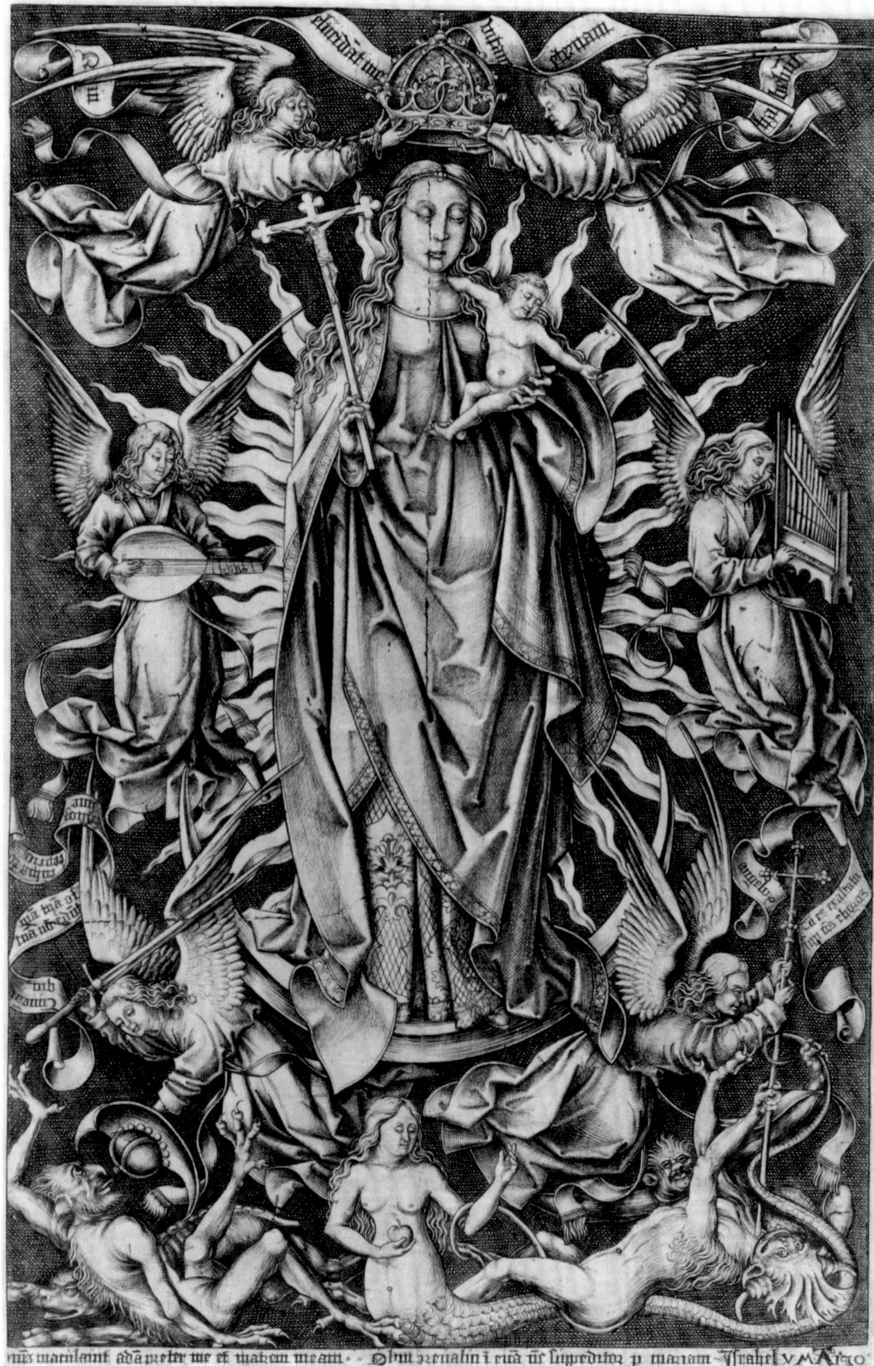

Figure 16. Israhel van Meckenem, *Virgin of the Apocalypse*, 1502. Engraving, 12 x 7⅔ in. (30.5 x 19.8 cm). Albertina Museum, Vienna (DG 1926/1091)

The architectonic solidity of the base contrasts, too, with the implied motion of the Virgin and Christ Child. Six angels with musical instruments support the base much in the same way as serenading angels often accompany Mary in heaven (fig. 16).[4] Two angels play psalteries (fig. 17), one of which is shown with two sound holes; another strums a lute; one plays a stringed instrument, perhaps a guitar or fiddle; another plucks a harp; and the identification of the now-lost instrument held by the final angel is unknown. The harp appears in the 1885 photograph, but is now missing. Two horizontal bands of grapevines, a reference to the Eucharist, frame the open, Gothic-style tracery (fig. 18) that ornaments a hollow compartment in the base, which may once have contained a holy relic. Sometimes relics were prominently displayed behind a piece of crystal or seen through an opening (see fig. 52).[5] Yet often relics were not shown, as the mere knowledge of their presence was sufficient. Here, any relics would have been wrapped in parchment or cloth, marked with an authenticating tag, and placed

Figure 17. *The Kimbell Virgin and Child*, angel playing a psaltery

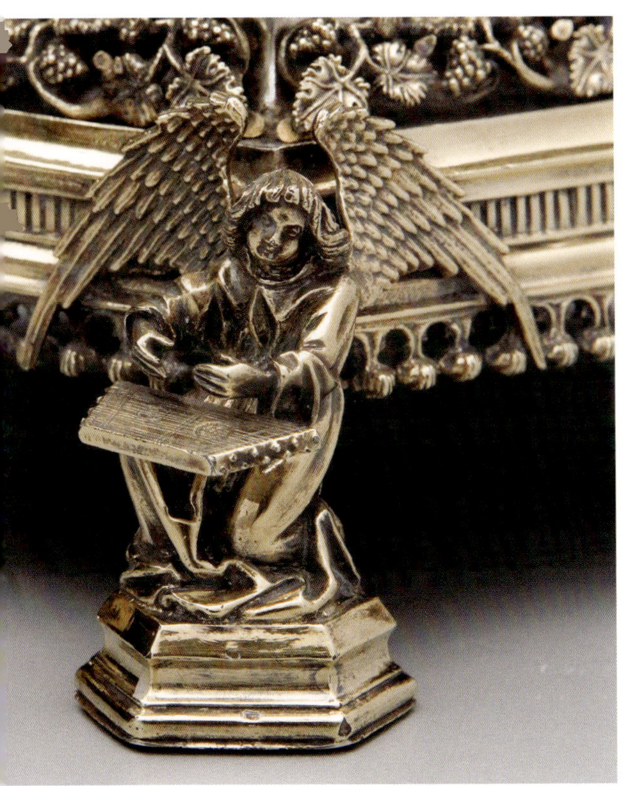

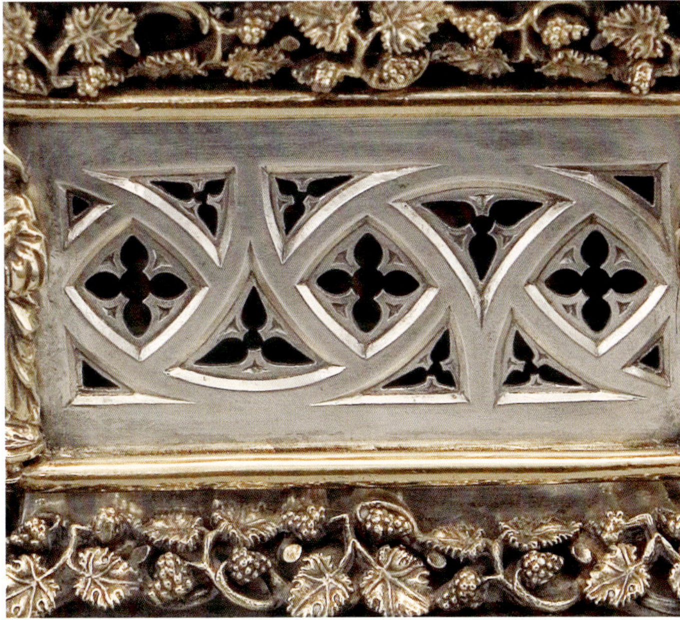

Figure 18. Gothic-style tracery panel

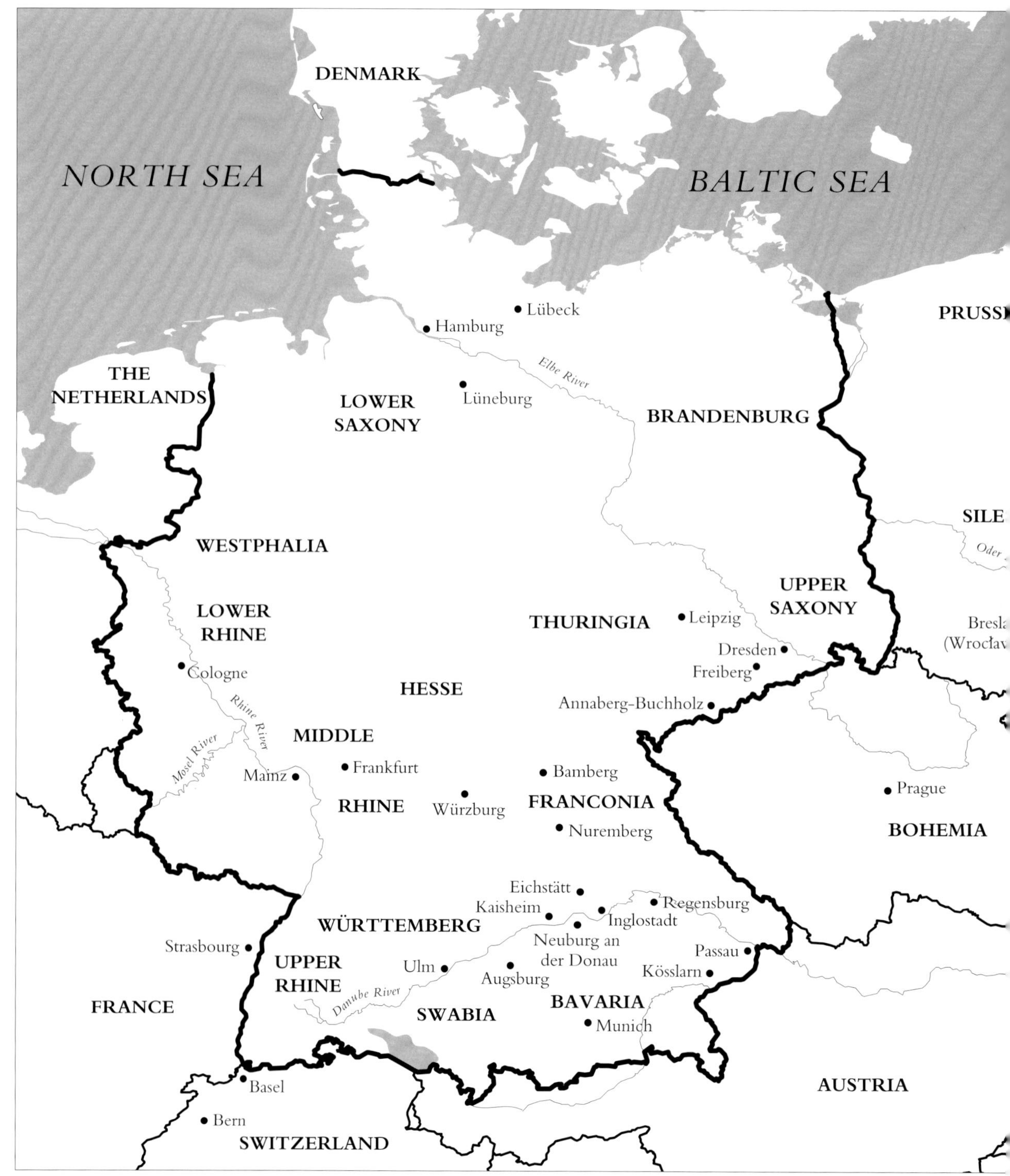

Figure 19. Map of Germany and parts of the Holy Roman Empire

within the compartment, which is accessible only by dismantling the base. On the underside of each leg on which the angels stand is a large, threaded screw sleeve. This indicates that the base originally was attached by screws to a larger wooden or metallic support, presumably to provide greater stability when placed on an altar.

Finally, six diminutive saints associated with Eichstätt and with Bishop Wilhelm flank these tracery panels. The small bishopric of Eichstätt is located in southern Franconia about midway between Augsburg and Nuremberg (fig. 19).[6] The town itself lies in the beautiful valley of the Altmühl River, surrounded by limestone hills (see fig. 25). According to episcopal history, Richard, an English noble who was often referred to as an Anglo-Saxon king, came to Eichstätt with his three children.[7] On the statuette, Richard, shown crowned (fig. 20), is accompanied by his sons Willibald and Wunibald, and

Figure 20. *The Kimbell Virgin and Child*, King Richard

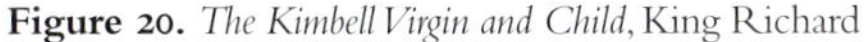

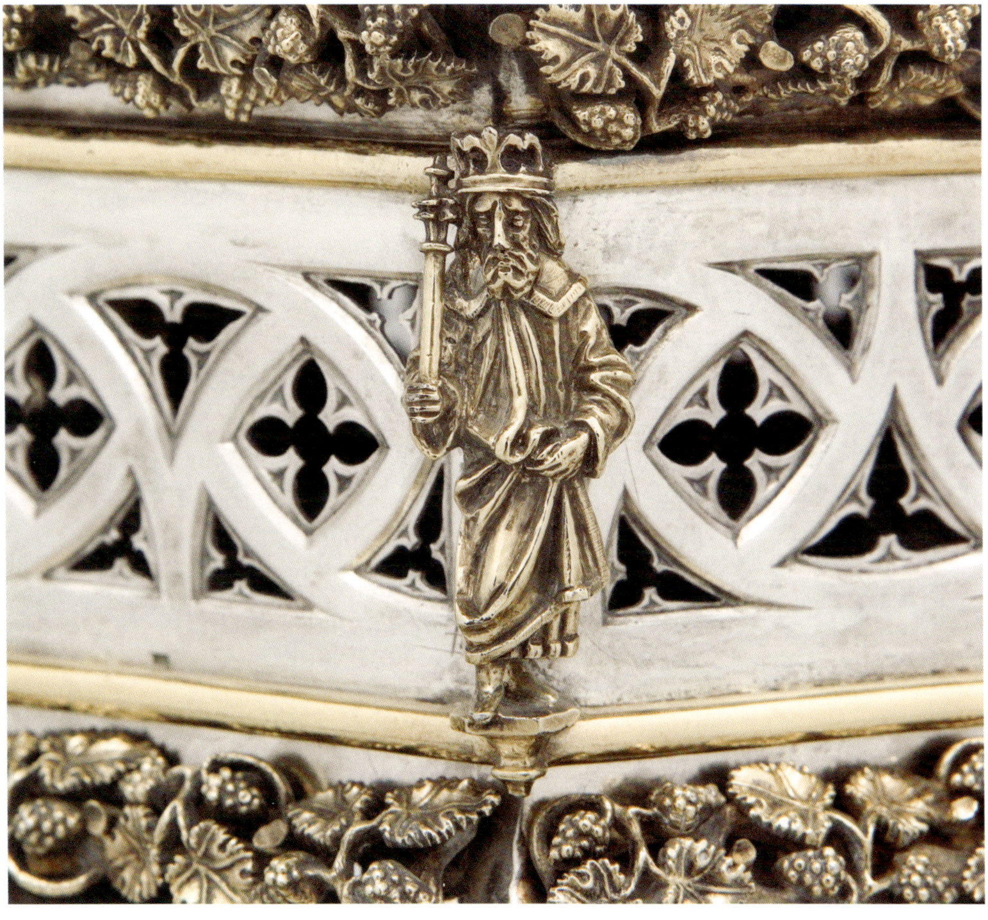

his daughter Walburga (figs. 21, 22). Willibald, Eichstätt's first bishop (r. 742–87) and, later, the diocese's main patron saint, is enshrined in the cathedral (see fig. 60). Wunibald and Walburga were respectively abbot and abbess of Heidenheim, a Benedictine monastery for both men and women, founded in 752 north of Eichstätt. Bishop Wilhelm venerated these four saints, who are commonly paired in local art (see figs. 66, 69). In 1484, he ordered new gravestones for Saints Wunibald and Walburga. In 1492, the bishop sent two of his trusted canons to England. They presented relics of Saints Richard, Willibald, and Walburga to King Henry VII (r. 1485–1509), who donated them to Canterbury Cathedral.

The remaining two saints are John the Evangelist and William of Maleval, better known as William the Hermit. John's inclusion likely honors Wilhelm's mentor and predecessor, Bishop Johann von Eich (r. 1445–64). The final figure sports a walking staff and a pilgrim's shell on his hat (fig. 23). Normally these are the features of Saint James of Compostela. There is, however, a better identification: Wilhelm's name saint, William of Maleval (or Malavalle), a French saint who died in 1157.[8] Although some sources suggest he journeyed to Santiago de Compostela, the shrine of Saint James, Saint William's vita reports that after a career as a soldier, he traveled to Rome, where Pope Eugenius III (r. 1145–53) pardoned him for his misdeeds but imposed, as penance, a pilgrimage to Jerusalem. Upon

Figure 21. Back of base with angels and saints

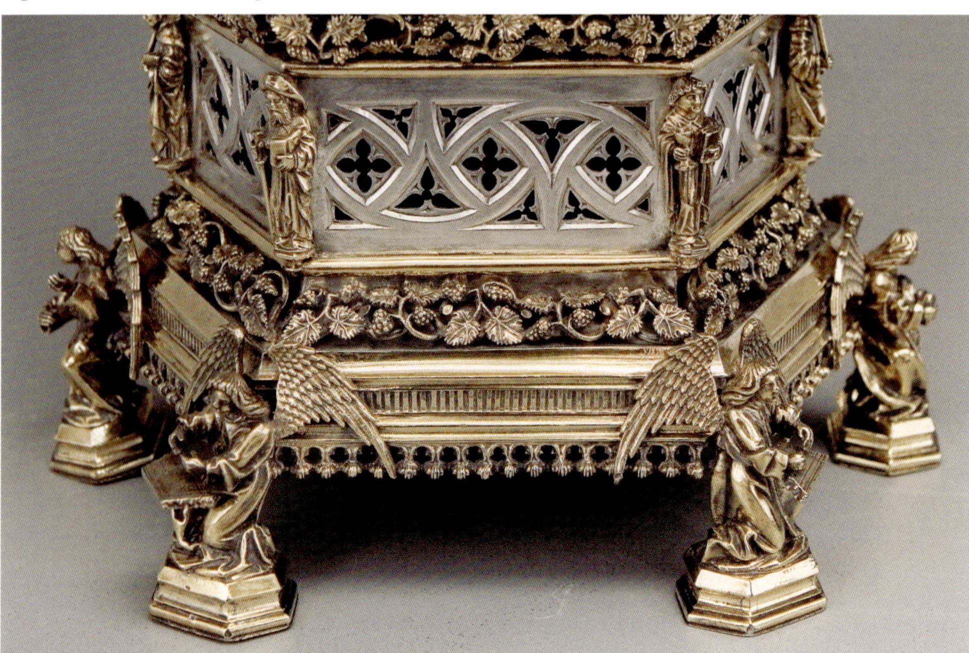

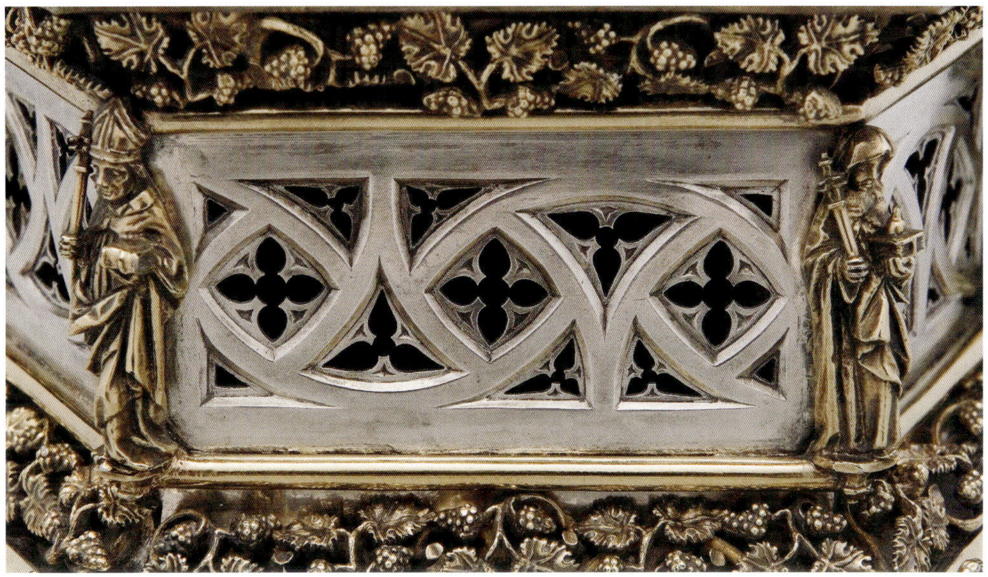

Figure 22. Saints Willibald (left) and Walburga (right)

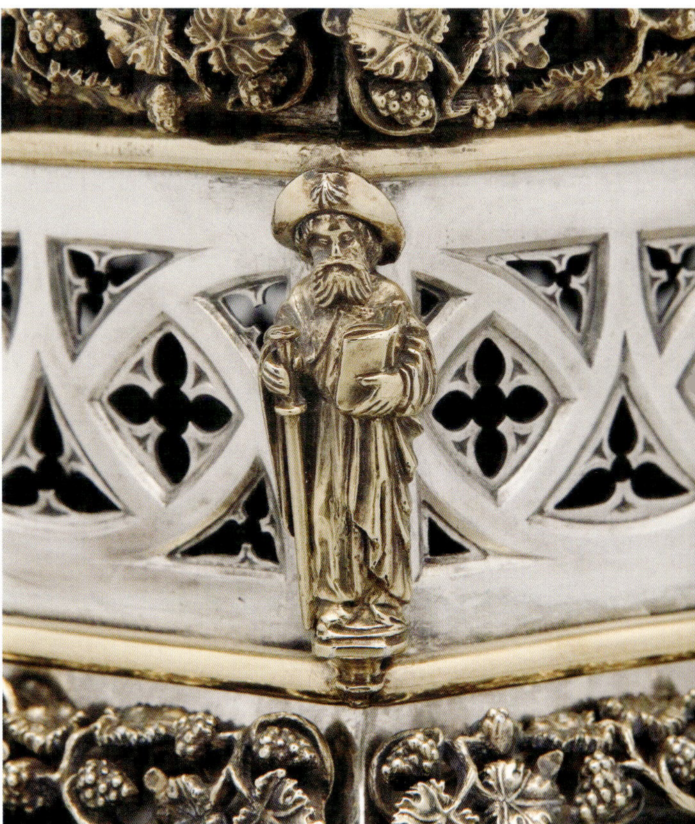

Figure 23. Saint William

Figure 24. Underside of base, dated 1486

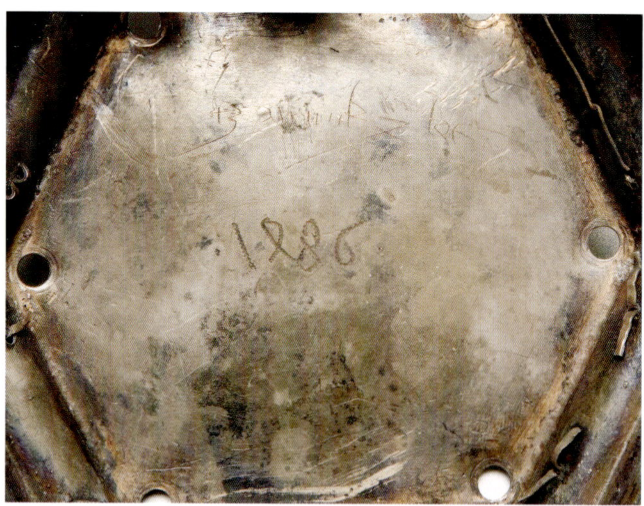

returning, he settled as a hermit near Pisa and in 1155 moved to a remote cave in a valley (Malavalle) near Siena. His followers formed a congregation known as the Gulielmites or the Hermits of Saint William. Pope Innocent III (r. 1198–1216) canonized him in 1202. Saint William stands behind Bishop Wilhelm on the bishop's tomb in the Willibald's, or western, choir of the cathedral (see fig. 56).

Two additional physical clues are invaluable for documenting the statuette. The date 1486, written in Gothic script, is incised into the underside of the base (fig. 24). This signals either the date of the statuette's completion or, less likely, its donation. Two identical coats of arms, one with color (red, silver, black, and silver bands) affixed to the front of the plinth and one engraved on the back side, belong to the patron, Bishop Wilhelm von Reichenau (see figs. 5, 13). Unfortunately, the statuette bears no punchmarks stamped into the metal that might identify the artist or the city of production.

An Artistic Moment in Time

The reign of Bishop Wilhelm von Reichenau, from 1464 to 1496, witnessed remarkable cultural and artistic developments. His world was rapidly expanding. In 1486 the Portuguese sailed around the Cape of Good Hope, at the southern tip of Africa. Six years later Christopher Columbus's voyage to the American Indies altered Europe's geographic horizons and its historical view that the world was divided into just three continents: Europe, Africa, and Asia. Of more immediate consequence was

Johann Gutenberg's publication of his 42-line Bible in Mainz, in 1456.[9] While Wilhelm was then just a university student in Erfurt, he would soon embrace this new technology in his diocese. As bishop, he would commission both unique, handwritten manuscripts and printed books. The invention of movable type revolutionized the written word and its use, since texts now could be printed in multiple copies. Before the end of the fifteenth century, thousands of religious and secular books appeared across the continent. Readership grew exponentially as literacy rates, most notably in cities, increased dramatically. Germany, as the cradle of publishing, took the lead, especially in Augsburg, Nuremberg, and Ulm, Eichstätt's neighbors.

Consider the intellectual, artistic, and commercial enterprise of the *Liber Chronicarum*, or *Nuremberg Chronicle*.[10] In 1493 Hartmann Schedel's chronicle of the world from its creation to the present was published by Anton Koberger in Nuremberg. Already in 1487–88, Schedel, the project's patrician financial backers, Koberger, and artists Michael Wolgemut and Wilhelm Pleydenwurff contracted to create an incunabula of unprecedented ambition, a large printed book that rivaled a richly illuminated manuscript. Published in a Latin edition of fifteen hundred and a German edition of one thousand copies, the *Nuremberg Chronicle* appealingly weds text and image. Wolgemut and his workshop prepared 645 different woodblocks, some of which were printed more than once for a total of 1,809 woodcut illustrations. These ranged from two-page city views to "portraits" of famous biblical and historical figures. The extant advertisement for this book reads in part, "I venture to promise you, reader, so great delight in reading it that you will think you are not reading a series of stories, but look at them with your own eyes. For you will see there not only portraits of emperors, popes, philosophers, poets, and other famous men each shown in the proper dress of his time, but also views of the most famous cities and places throughout Europe.... Farewell, and do not let this book slip through your hands."[11] Among the images is the earliest known depiction of Eichstätt (fig. 25). Beneath representations of Saints Willibald and Walburga, the view encompasses the walled city with the twin-towered cathedral and, just below, Wilhelm von Reichenau's episcopal palace marked with his coat of arms. The bishop's fortress, the Willibaldsburg, looms above the town. Koberger, Nuremberg's foremost publisher, reportedly employed one hundred workers and owned twenty-four presses. He also developed an efficient network of sales agents across Europe, so that this and other books truly reached an international audience.

In 1486, the year inscribed on the bottom of the *Kimbell Virgin and Child*, Albrecht Dürer entered Wolgemut's workshop as an apprentice. He had already been partially trained by his father, Albrecht the Elder, a goldsmith. The young artist, who likely designed some of the *Nuremberg Chronicle*'s woodcuts, was deeply impressed by the aesthetic and commercial possibilities of prints. Within just a few years, Dürer's woodcuts and engravings made him Europe's best-known artist. In 1498, using the presses and distribution system of Koberger, who was his godfather, Dürer published *The Apocalypse*.[12]

S. wilibaldus epus

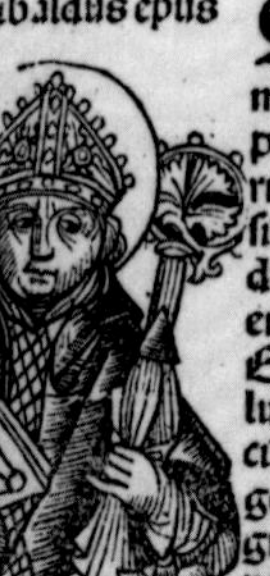

S. walpurgis

Sanctus wilibaldus natus e ex sancto richardo sue
uox duce. atq; anglox rege. Bunnaq; castissima se
mina eius vxore. Qui cu hierosolimã atq; terrã sanctam
peregrinus visitasset. z indç romam reuertisset. a grego
rio tercõ summo põtifice. Cui tuz ppter religionë tũ fidei
sinceritatez dilectus fuit. sancto bonifacio maguntine se/
dis archiepiscopo cõmendatur. z a sancto Bonifacio (q
eius auũculus fuit).xj.kal'. Augusti presbiter ordinaf.
Et thuringie in loco cui Sulzpurg vocabulũ est anno sa
lutis.740. sue vo etatis.41. episcopio Eystetensi presi
citur. qd sanctus bonifacius ex pdijs z mancipijs a swi/
gero comite deo dunatis erexerat. Efficitur etiã sedis ma
guntine scriba. quem vulgus cancellarium vocat. hocq;
priuilegio vtatur. vt ipe eiusq; successores officio scribe
sedis maguntine perpetuo fruantur. Et in concilijs z conuentibus a dextris archiepiscopi maguntii pri
mũ locum semper obtineant. accepit etiam vestem insignem. quã rationale vocant. Qua veteres sacerdo
tes vtebantur. vt ea etiam successores superuestiri liceret. Hic vir sanctus wilibaldus supra ripam flumi
nis quod alimoniũ vocatur. In vasta solitudine. succisis nemoxibus. ciuitatem Eystet edificare cepit. In
qua z monasterium sanctimonialiũ ordinis sancti benedicti celebre sarchophage sancte walpurgis virgi
nis admirabilis. que fuit soroz sancti wilibaldi. De cuius reliquijs manat sacer liquox. egrotantibus pre
bens remedium. Nũc presidet ecclesie eystetensi que z aureatensis nũcupatur. presul dignissimus wilbel
mus oxtus ex nobili familia reichenawç.

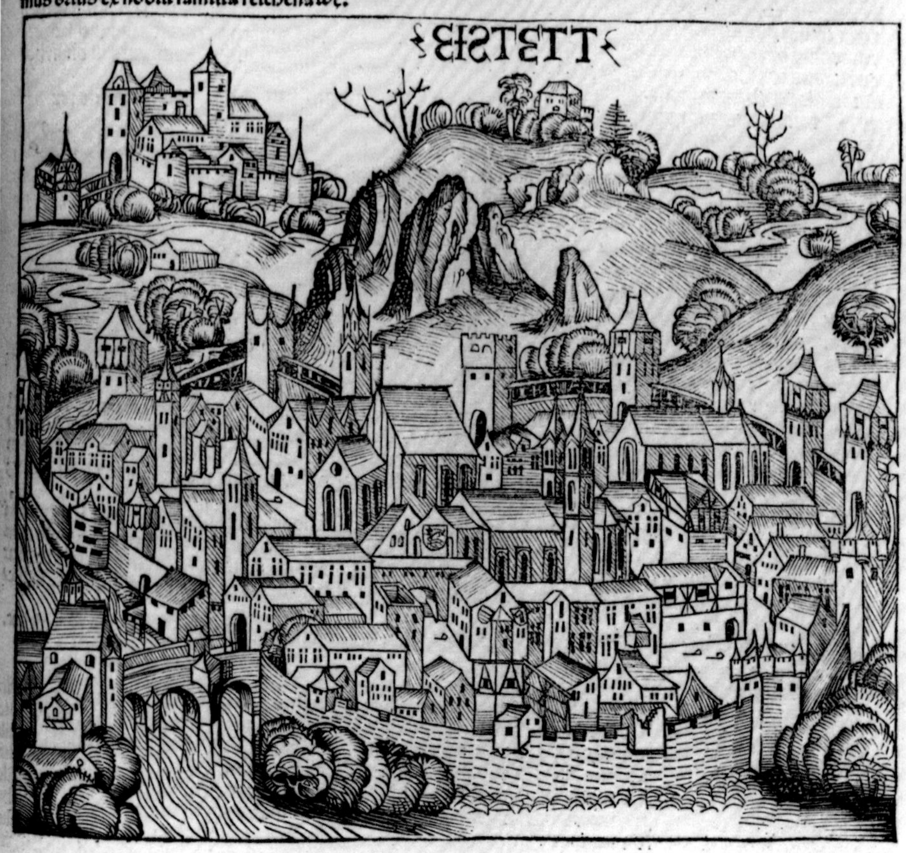

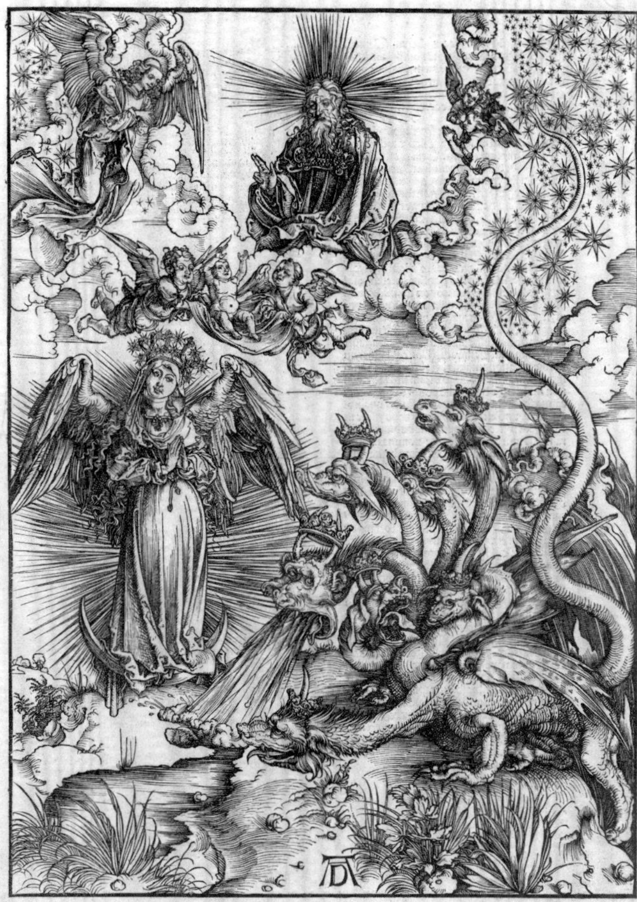

Figure 26. Albrecht Dürer, *Virgin of the Apocalypse with the Seven-Headed Beast*, c. 1497, from *The Apocalypse.* Nuremberg: Albrecht Dürer, 1498. Woodcut, 15⁷⁄₁₆ x 11 in. (39.2 x 27.9 cm). Museum of Fine Arts, Boston, Gift of Edward P. Warren (M9414)

The text, available in either Latin or German, appears on the page facing each of the fifteen full-page woodcuts. Although the subject matter had considerable appeal as the year 1500 loomed, with its millennial fears, it was Dürer's technical and compositional virtuosity that secured the publication's extraordinary success. In the ninth woodcut, the Virgin standing on a crescent moon hovers above the earth (fig. 26). The horrific seven-headed beast approaches her, but before it can devour her newborn son, the child is carried safely to heaven by two angels. The Virgin's beauty and humility are exquisitely contrasted with the hideousness of the diabolic beast.

Figure 25. Michael Wolgemut and Wilhelm Pleydenwurff, *View of Eichstätt*, from Hartmann Schedel's *Liber Chronicarum [Nuremberg Chronicle]*. Nuremberg: Anton Koberger, 1493. Woodcut, 8⅛ x 9 in. (20.5 x 22.8 cm). Harry Ransom Humanities Research Center, The University of Texas at Austin (Incun 1493 S32, fol. 162 recto). The building in the front center marked with two coats of arms is the former bishop's palace built by Wilhelm.

Dürer, Martin Schongauer, and Israhel van Meckenem, among other German masters, stoked the ever-growing demand for religious and secular prints on both sides of the Alps. Their attractive images appealed to a broad audience.[13] Some valued prints for their subjects, especially those with devotional content (see figs. 16, 70). Many artists bought prints as a handy visual repertory of iconographic and design models (see fig. 34). Still others collected prints for their own aesthetic merits.

During Bishop Wilhelm's reign, much of European art addressed religious themes. Following the death of Rogier van der Weyden in 1464, Hugo van der Goes of Ghent and Hans Memling, a German artist residing in Bruges, emerged as the most influential painters in the Netherlands. Van der Goes's monumental triptych of the *Adoration of the Shepherds* (fig. 27), better known as the Portinari Altarpiece, was created in about 1473–78 for Tommaso Portinari, the Medici bank's representative in Bruges.[14] Perhaps as a token of his personal success in a foreign land and his family's historical support

Figure 27. Hugo van der Goes, *Adoration of the Shepherds* (Portinari Altarpiece), central panel, c. 1473–78. Oil on panel, 98 x 119¹¹⁄₁₆ in. (249 x 304 cm). Galleria degli Uffizi, Florence

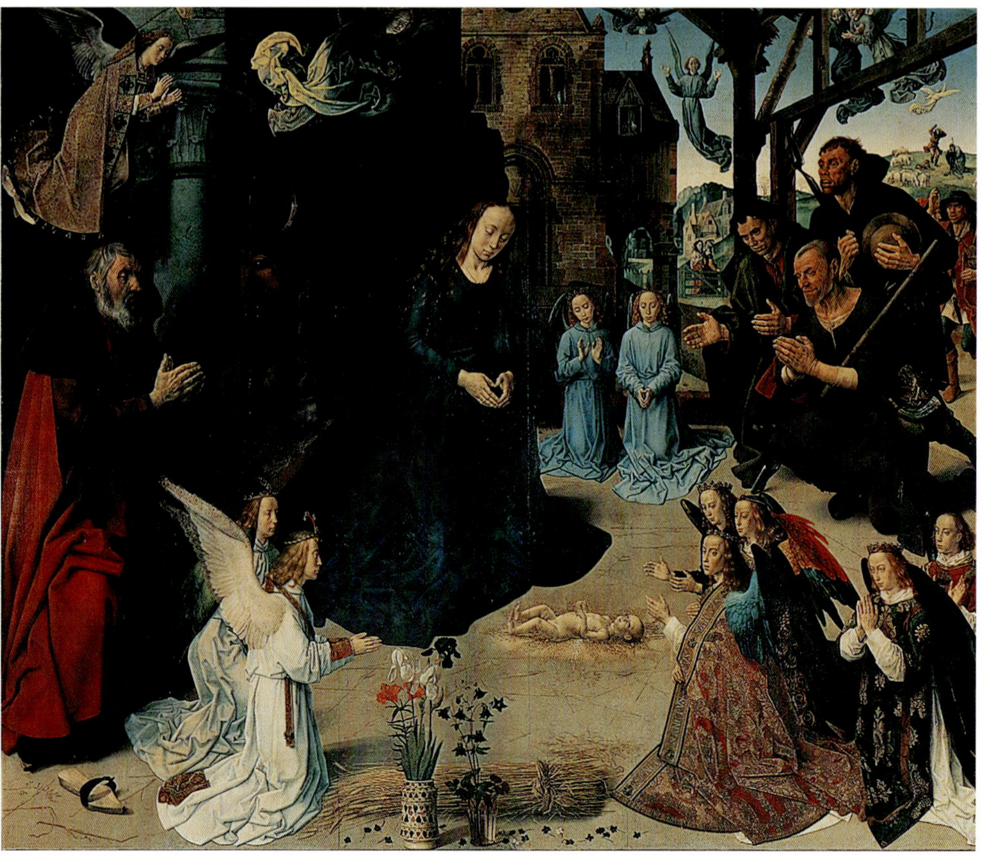

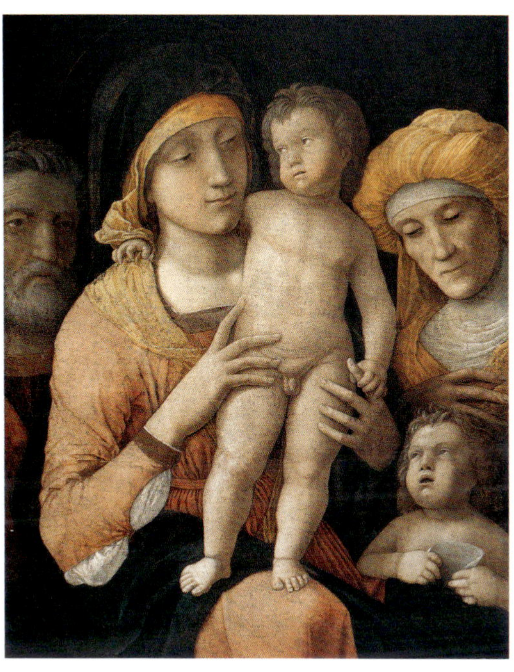

Figure 28. Andrea Mantegna, *The Madonna and Child with Saints Joseph, Elizabeth, and John the Baptist*, c. 1485–88. Distemper, oil, and gold on canvas, 24¾ x 20¼ in. (62.9 x 51.3 cm). Kimbell Art Museum, Fort Worth

for this church, Portinari sent the winged retable to his native Florence, where in 1483 it was placed on the high altar of Sant'Egidio in the hospital of Santa Maria Nuova. The intense colors and meticulous naturalism had another purpose besides revealing the artist's virtuosity. Many of the objects in the central panel are charged with symbolic meaning. Contemporaries would have recognized features such as the columbine, carnations, and violets as references to Mary's humility and sorrows, or the three irises and the scarlet lily as signifiers of Christ's passion, purity, and royalty. The shaft of wheat alludes to the Eucharist, while the angels wear liturgical vestments appropriate for assisting a new priest, Christ, performing his first divine Mass. This combination of the real and the symbolic is highly characteristic of Netherlandish art. To this, however, van der Goes adds a spiritual dimension. Mary is almost melancholic as she ponders both the miraculous birth and sacrificial future of her son. This somber, reflective mood of the onlookers signals the growing influence of the Modern Devotion, an ascetic movement that urged Christians to deepen their personal faith through meditative consideration of and empathetic identification with Christ and his mother. Van der Goes became a lay brother in a Windesheim monastery outside of Brussels shortly after finishing this painting.

Andrea Mantegna's *Madonna and Child with Saints Joseph, Elizabeth, and John the Baptist* (fig. 28) in the Kimbell Art Museum compellingly shows the intense interest in the humanity of Christ and his family in contemporary Italian art.[15] This small painting, much like the *Kimbell Virgin and Child* statuette, is a private devotional object. Mantegna's tightly knit composition stresses the personal relationships and distinctive roles of each of the holy figures. Mary gently holds her standing son on her lap. They tenderly stare at each other. Christ grasps her left index finger more for reassurance than for balance. The position of Mary's hands draws attention to Christ's maleness, a common feature in art that signals the fulfillment of prophesy that the Word has been made flesh; that is, that God has assumed human form.[16] Joseph, set apart in the shadows, looks on somberly. Meanwhile, Elizabeth, Mary's elderly cousin, stares pensively at her own son, John the Baptist. For his part, John looks up at Christ. He holds a blank text, as an allusion to his future prophetic words that Christ is the Son of God and the lamb that takes away the sins of the world (John 1). Mantegna's spare, half-length composition is stripped of all unessential features. The highly sculpturesque figures are beautifully modeled by the light and subtle coloration.

Figure 29. Sandro Botticelli, *The Birth of Venus*, c. 1484–86. Tempera and oil on canvas, 69 x 110 in. (175 x 279 cm). Galleria degli Uffizi, Florence

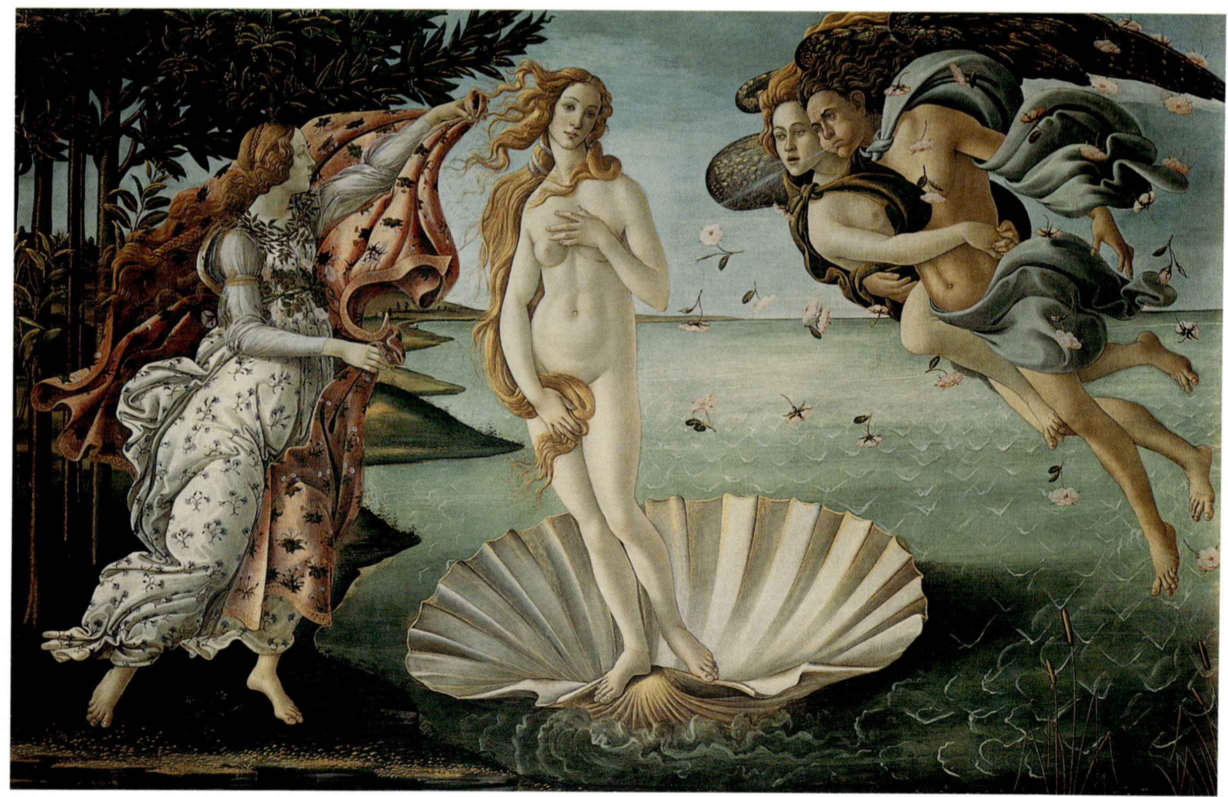

Although Mantegna, the ducal court painter for the Gonzagas in Mantua, is famous for his knowledge of ancient sculpture and linear perspective, hallmarks of Italian Renaissance art, his religious paintings reveal the same spirit that suffuses the Portinari Altarpiece and the *Kimbell Virgin and Child*. Artists adapted their styles according to the subjects or needs of specific projects. For example, Sandro Botticelli painted the famous *Birth of Venus* (fig. 29) in about 1484–86, contemporaneous with Bishop Wilhelm's statuette.[17] Inspired by classical sources and the writings of Marsilio Ficino, the Florentine humanist, the artist's lyrical picture shows Venus, the goddess of love, rising out of the sea. Her pose emulates the *Venus pudica*, or modest-Venus type, which was popular in ancient sculpture. Botticelli's painting, with its flat style, evokes a mythic, dreamlike world, not a naturalistic one.

The last third of the fifteenth century witnessed competing and often conflicting tendencies. Botticelli's Florence encompassed both the reign of Lorenzo the Magnificent, a munificent patron of the arts who died in 1492, and the ascetic Dominican Fra Girolamo Savanarola, who railed against the city and its luxury before being hung in 1498. Broad labels such as late medieval and Renaissance mean little, because for every classical-inspired edifice, such as the courtyard of the Ducal Palace (1465–72) in Urbino, one finds intricate Gothic-style structures, from Milan Cathedral and many of Venice's palaces to churches and town halls across northern Europe (see fig. 61). The highly refined *Kimbell Virgin and Child* would have fit comfortably into almost any European church or private devotional setting of this era.

The Art of the Goldsmith

The Kimbell statuette epitomizes the skill of the best Late-Gothic German goldsmiths. Modern tastes favor painting over other media. This distorts the historical position of goldsmiths, who were often the wealthiest and most privileged artists. Nuremberg's goldsmiths were sworn artists; that is, annually they literally promised not to travel outside the city without the council's permission and not to share trade secrets with colleagues in other towns.[18] Goldsmiths were critical to Nuremberg's economy due to the preciousness of their working materials, and, as a result, were tightly regulated. Painters and printmakers, including Albrecht Dürer, were categorized as free artists. Less economically vital, these masters enjoyed fewer restrictions but also less support from the city.

Goldsmiths produced a wide array of secular and religious works. Around 1503, a Nuremberg goldsmith created the *Schlüsselfelder Ship* for a local patrician (fig. 30). This silver table decoration is actually a practical wine decanter with a capacity of 2⅓ liters. Liquid pours from the dragon's mouth. Yet the realistic character of the ship, with its dozens of sailors and passengers, some engaged in amusing

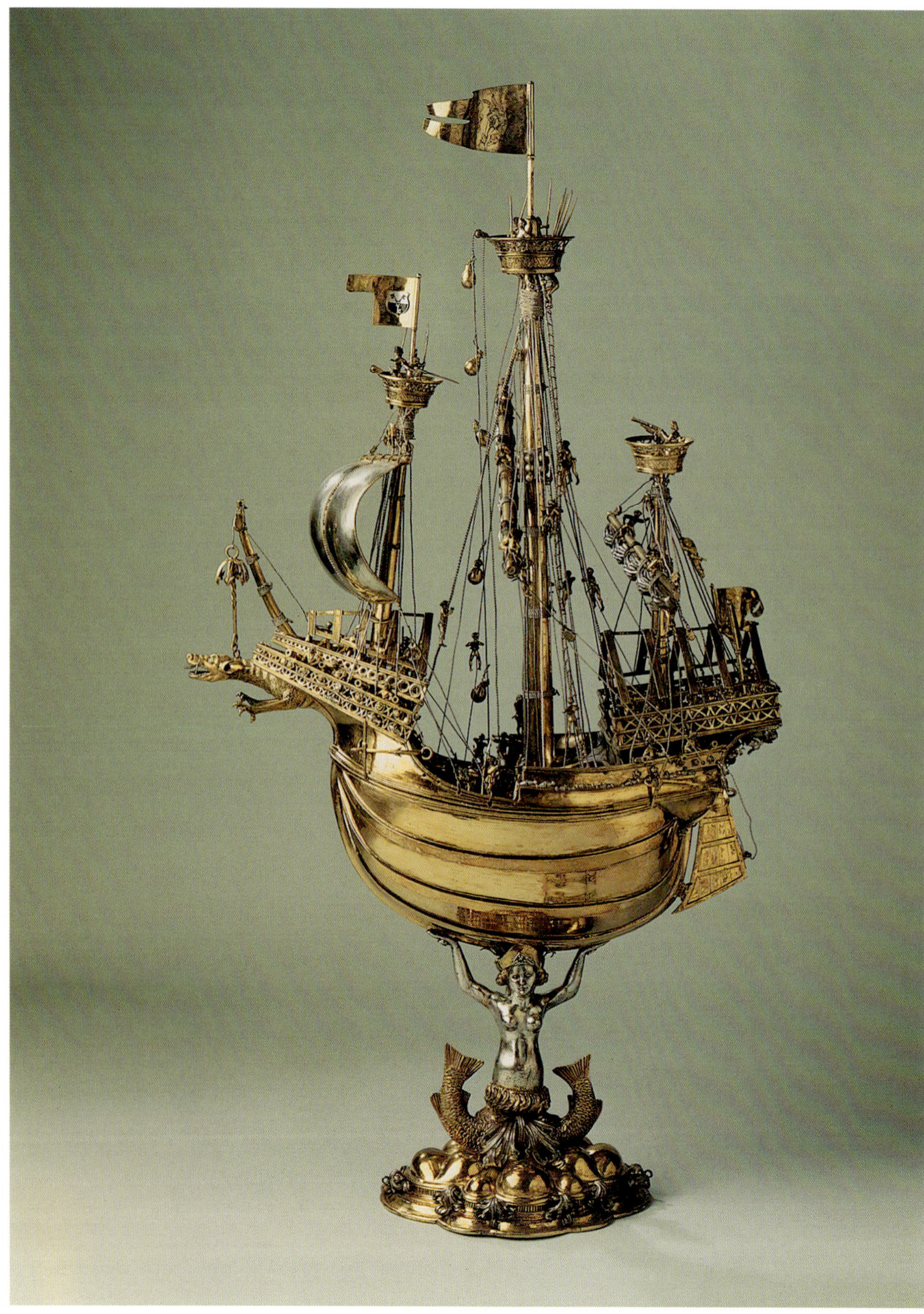

Figure 30. Nuremberg goldsmith, *Schlüsselfelder Ship*, 1503. Silver with gilt, 31¼ x 17¼ in. (79 x 43.5 cm). Germanisches Nationalmuseum, Nuremberg (HG 2146)

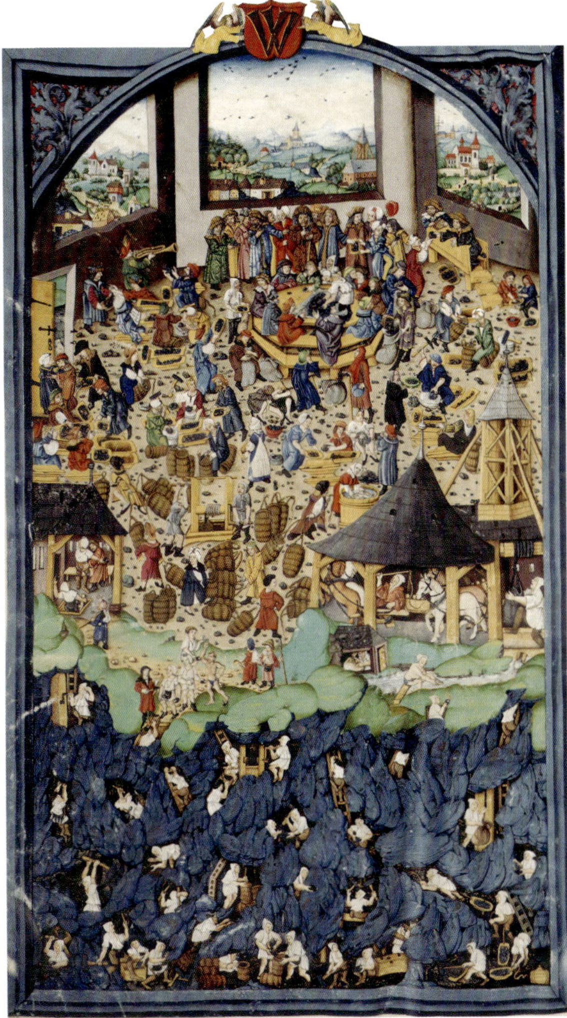

Figure 31. Matthaus of Kuttenberg, *Mine at Kutná Hora* (Kuttenberg), frontispiece of the *Kuttenberger Kanzional*, c. 1490. Miniature. Austrian National Library, Picture Archives, Vienna (MS Cod. 15.501, fol. 1 verso) (E 21.304-C)

or amorous activities, captivates our attention. The artistic sophistication of such works as this or the *Kimbell Virgin and Child* is obvious. Unfortunately, few high-quality goldsmith objects still exist. Scholar Johann Michael Fritz estimates that less than one half of 1 percent of goldsmith works from this period survive.[19] The aesthetic merits of a goldsmith piece were often weighed against its material worth. In times of war or economic need, silver objects were melted down as a form of liquid wealth.

Most of the high-quality silver used in south Germany was mined in the Tyrol, Bohemia, or southern Saxony. During the late fifteenth century, major discoveries of silver fueled the emergence of wealthy mining towns, such as Annaberg, on the border between Saxony and Bohemia. A contemporary miniature portrays a mine at Kutná Hora (Kuttenberg), east of Prague (fig. 31).[20] The miners, dressed in lightweight white clothes, cut the ore from the seams beneath the ground and hoist it to the

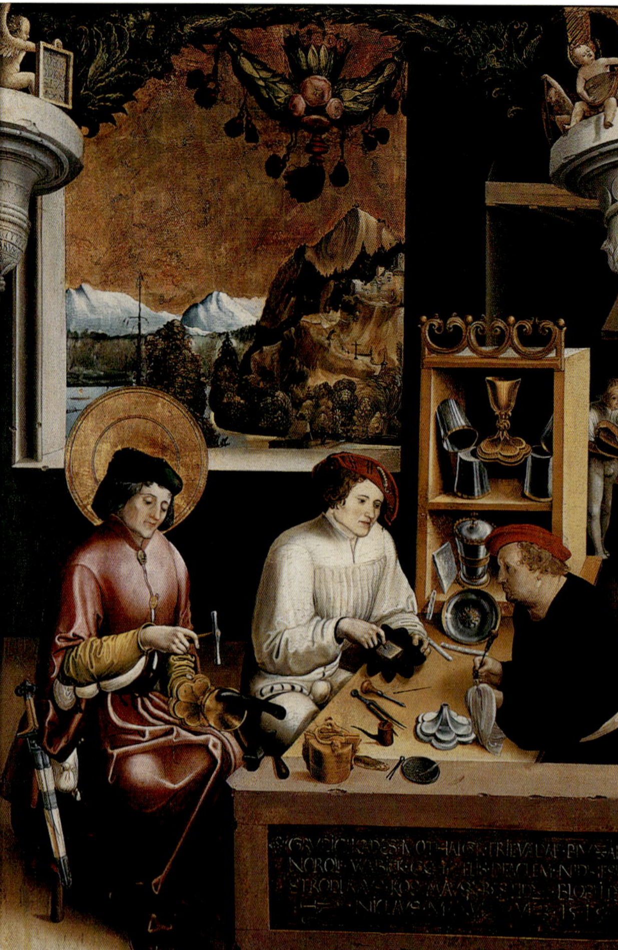

Figure 32. Niklaus Manuel Deutsch, *Saint Eligius in His Workshop*, panel of the Mary Altar, originally made for the chapel of the Painters and Goldsmiths' Guild in the Dominican church in Bern, 1515. Oil on pine panel, 47⁷⁄₁₆ x 32¾ in. (120.5 x 83.3 cm). Kunstmuseum Bern, Burgergemeinde Bern (G2020B)

surface using pulleys. The ore was then crushed and processed to separate the silver from base metals and rock. The silver was then graded. Silver mined near Freiberg in Saxony was renowned for its purity and mushy texture. The silver was purified, melted into plates or bricks, and shipped. Once at its final destination, it was then remelted and formed into sheets.

Niklaus Manuel Deutsch illustrates a contemporary goldsmith's workshop in his panel of Saint Eligius or Eloi (c. 588–660), the patron saint of goldsmiths (fig. 32).[21] Sitting at his workbench, Eligius carefully hammers a chalice or drinking cup on a curved anvil. A very full purse signals his financial success. The older assistant at right, likely a journeyman, holds a ring tightly in a cloth as he engraves its surface. Another helper incises a decoration on a small piece of metal nestled in a cushion. He will rotate the pillow so that his hand can always work the metal away from his body. On the ledge and table are a second hammer, a large brass container with a set of weights, a rabbit's foot, tweezers, a small bowl with a borax pap, the silver base of a future cup or dish, an oil can with borax, a compass, engraving burin, and a nail file. Borax was used as a fireproofing agent. A gilt chalice, four cups, a covered cup and dish, and pieces of crystal with rings are displayed in the nearby case. Behind, an apprentice uses a bellows to stoke the fire needed to melt metal.

Rules about the number and type of workers in any goldsmith's shop varied from town to town.[22] A master goldsmith sometimes worked with other masters. More commonly, a goldsmith had one or two journeymen or skilled assistants. These are either workers who spent a year or two in other cities completing their training or craftsmen with special talents, paid daily, who did not aspire to be or were earning money to become independent masters. The goldsmith would house, feed, and educate one or two apprentices who might take four to eight years learning the trade.

A goldsmith's shop typically possessed a stock of designs for its use and for showing prospective customers. In 1578 Basilius Amerbach, a wealthy Basel collector, purchased the entire contents, including tools, of the Schweiger family's atelier.[23] Most of the 773 goldsmith models and 709 drawings and prints once belonged to Jörg Schweiger of Augsburg, who worked in Basel from 1507 to 1533. These designs ranged from sketches for foliage patterns to detailed studies of statuettes, reliquaries, monstrances, and other related objects. Jörg(?)'s *Saint Christopher* statuette on a hexagonal base is conceptually akin to the *Kimbell Virgin and Child* (fig. 33).[24] Many German engravers learned to use the burin and work with copper during their own training as goldsmiths. High-quality prints by

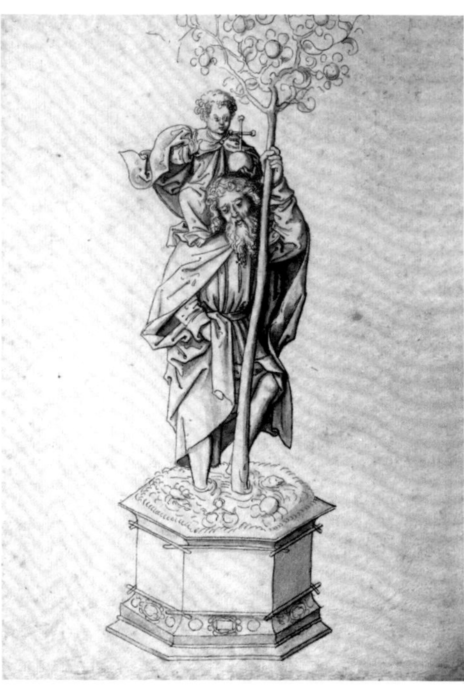

Figure 33. Attributed to Jörg Schweiger, copy after an Augsburg artist, *Design for a Saint Christopher Statuette*, before 1493 (original). Drawing in pen and wash, 8½ x 6 in. (21.6 x 15.2 cm). Kunstmuseum Basel, Kupferstichkabinett (U.VIII.45)

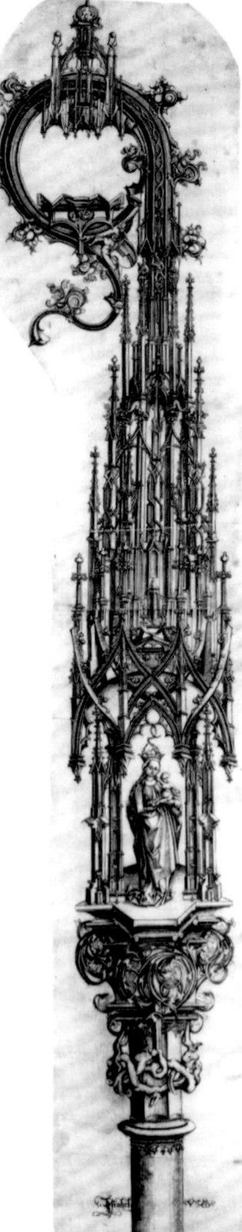

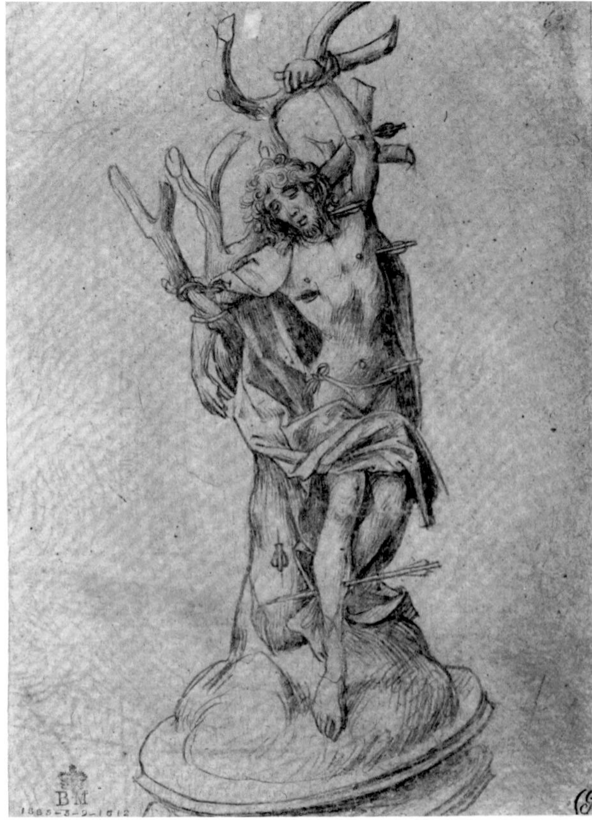

Figure 34. Israhel van Meckenem, *Bishop's Crozier*, 1490s (?). Engraving using two plates, upper 14¾ x 6½ in. (37.4 x 16.5 cm); lower 15¹¹⁄₁₆ x 4⅞ in. (39.9 x 12.3 cm). Kunstmuseum Basel, Kupferstichkabinett (K.VIII.18)

Figure 35. Hans Holbein the Elder, *Saint Sebastian*, by 1497. Metalpoint drawing, 5⅙ x 3¾ in. (13.1 x 9.6 cm). The Trustees of the British Museum, London (1885-5-9-1612 verso)

Master E.S., Martin Schongauer, and Israhel van Meckenem, among others, were avidly collected by other artists for their repertory of compositional and thematic ideas. Van Meckenem's *Bishop's Crozier* is a masterpiece of micro-architecture and Gothic-style ornament (fig. 34).[25] The general similarities between its central Virgin and Child and the Kimbell statuette reveal that both are grounded in a common type rather than any direct association. Engravers borrowed pictorial ideas from other media and, in turn, quickly disseminated these across the German-speaking lands.

The creation of a complex silver statuette is a collaborative endeavor. A painter, sculptor, or goldsmith prepared an initial design. Augsburg artist Hans Holbein the Elder's drawing for a *Saint*

Sebastian statuette is fairly summary, yet it offers a clear sense of the saint's contorted pose and physical anguish (fig. 35).[26] Next a sculptor or goldsmith often would carve a full-scale wooden model based on the drawing. If a model had been prepared for this project, it either has not been identified or does not survive. The model for the final silver statuette, made for Georg Kastner, abbot (r. 1490–1509) of the Cistercian monastery at Kaisheim, near Donauwörth and just south of the Eichstätt diocese, does (fig. 36).[27] The anonymous Augsburg goldsmith followed Holbein's design closely, as evident in the saint's pose or how the cloak sweeps around the tree and across the body. The goldsmith altered some of the branches and reconfigured the ground beneath Sebastian's feet. He added features such as veining in the saint's arms and legs, more articulated facial details, and a new base.

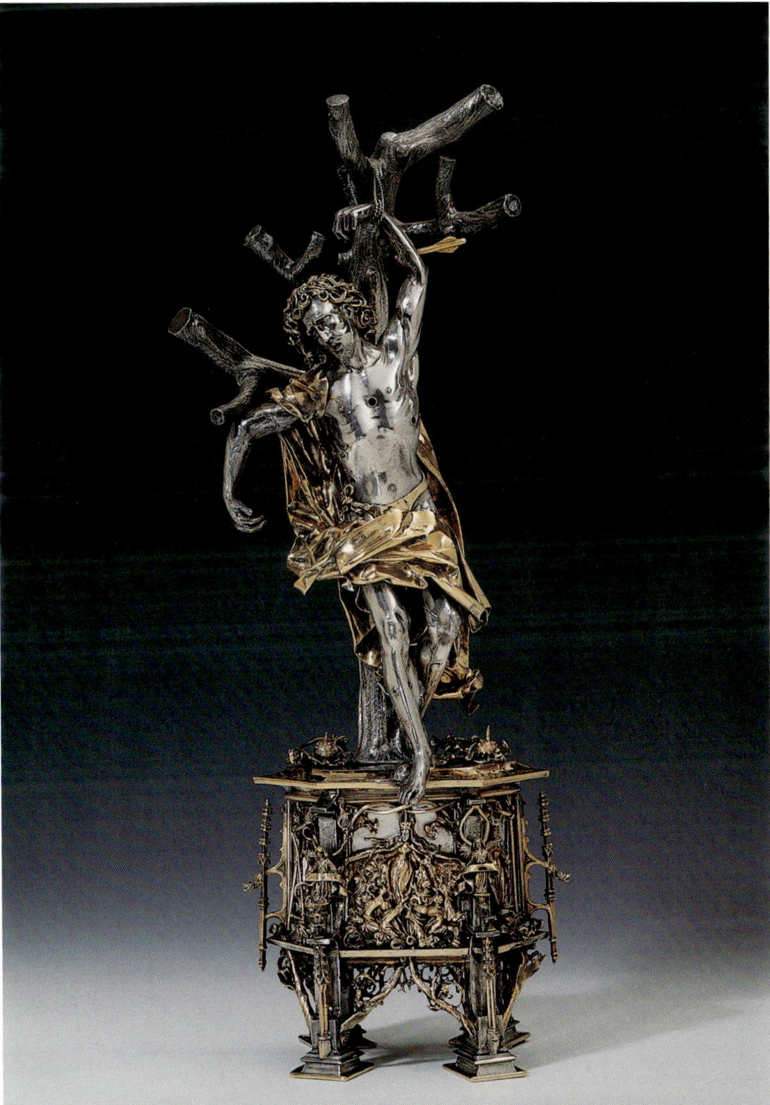

Figure 36. Augsburg goldsmith, *Saint Sebastian*, 1497. Silver with gilt, figure 10⅝ in. (27 cm); figure with base 19½ in. (49.5 cm). V&A Images/Victoria and Albert Museum, London (M.27-2001)

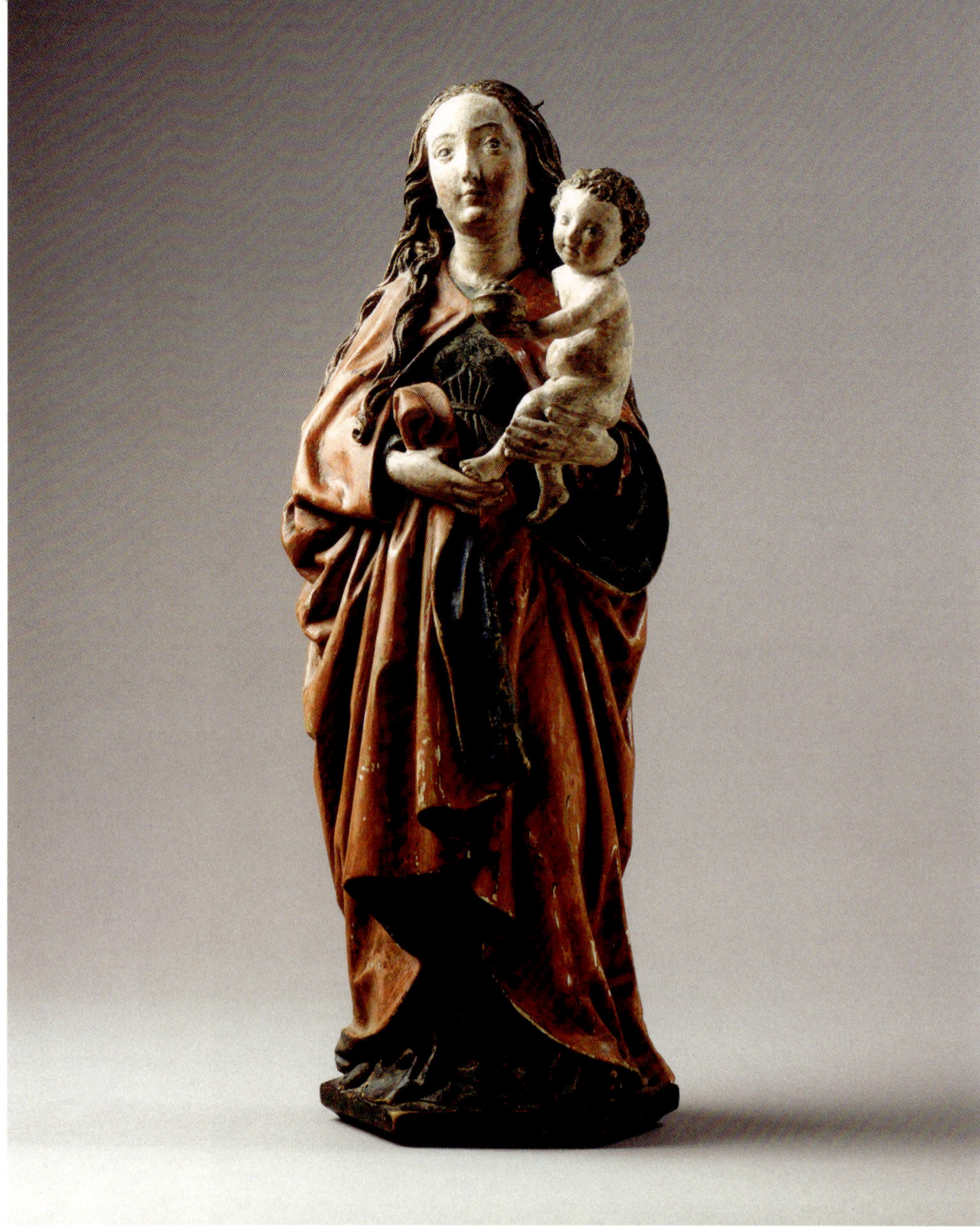

Figure 37. Attributed to Michel Erhart and workshop, *Virgin and Child*, c. 1480. Lindenwood with mainly modern polychrome, 15³⁄₁₆ x 5½ in. (38.5 x 14 cm). Private collection, Vienna

Neither a drawing nor wooden model exist for the *Kimbell Virgin and Child*. Indeed, few comparable wooden models survive or, at least, have been identified. The closest association is the limewood *Virgin and Child* attributed to Michel Erhart of Ulm and Heinrich Hufnagel's silver statuette (figs. 37, 38).[28] According to the inscription on the latter's base, Hufnagel, an Augsburg goldsmith, made it in 1482 for Abbot Johannes Fisches of Kaisheim (r. 1479–90).[29] Although he carefully mimicked the poses and drapery patterns of the wooden statue, the goldsmith freely modified details and likely

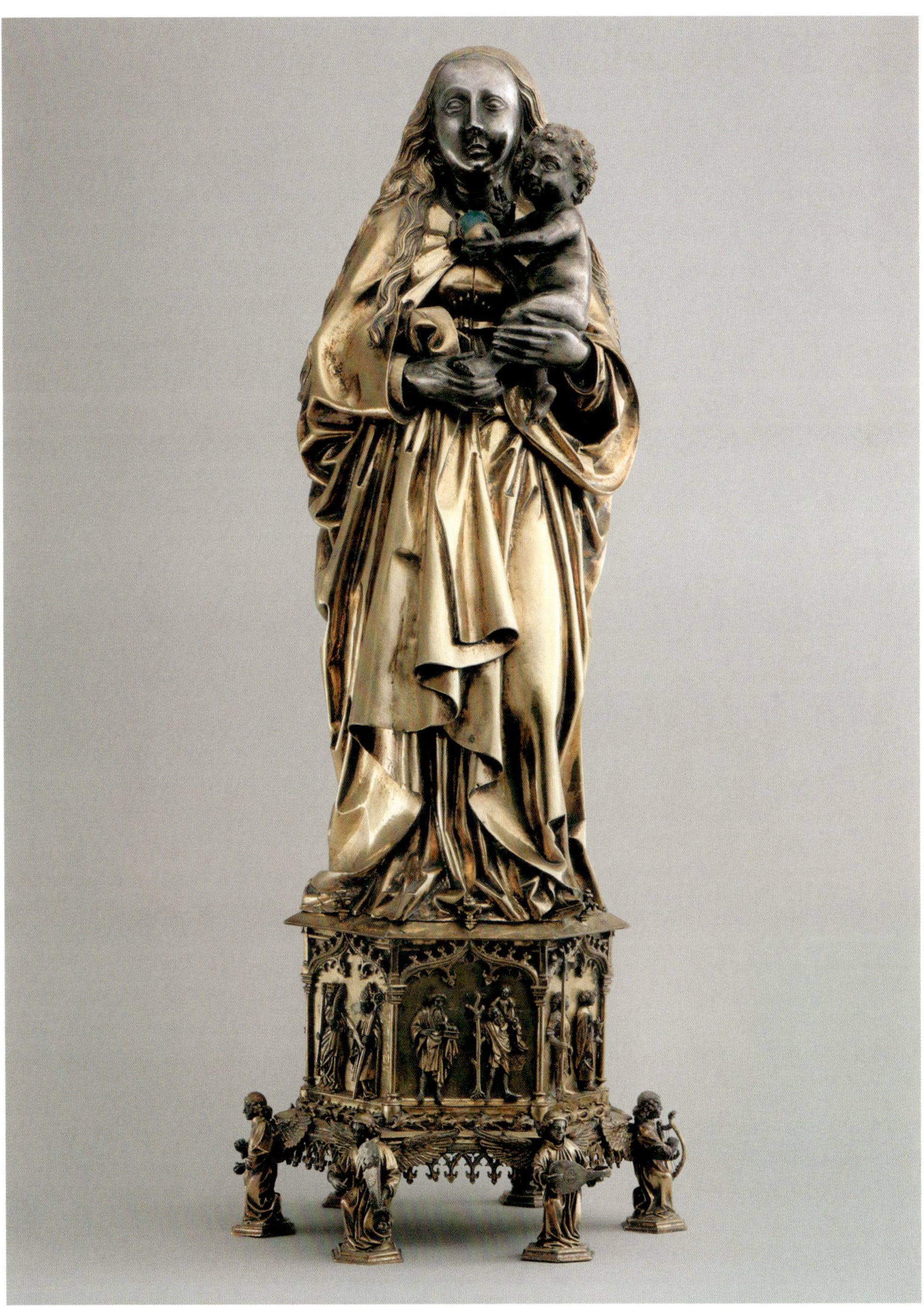

Figure 38. Heinrich Hufnagel, *Virgin and Child*, 1482. Silver with gilt, 14⁹⁄₁₆ x 5¹³⁄₁₆ in. (37 x 14.8 cm); height with base 19⅞ in. (50.5 cm). Skulpturensammlung und Museum für Byzantinische Kunst, Staatliche Museen, Berlin (773)

devised the base. Hufnagel's Christ is positioned more vertically, Mary's drapery folds are a bit flatter, and the reflective metallic surfaces are handled differently than the polychromed wood. Erhart(?)'s model provided the basic design. It was not used for casting nor as a form against which the metal could be beaten.

Let us consider how the *Kimbell Virgin and Child* was made. It is hollow, to minimize its cost and weight as well as to facilitate its production. Soon after its purchase by the Kimbell Art Museum, the statuette was examined by conservator Peter Dandridge, who disassembled its four basic parts (crown, figures with plinth, and the upper and lower halves of the base) to permit close scrutiny (figs. 39, 40; see fig. 78).[30] The Virgin is formed using three sheets of silver: one for her back; a second for her face, neck, and the upper part of her dress; and a third for her draped body and the face of the moon. These sheets are joined on the interior by a series of silver tabs fitted into silver posts on the adjoining sheets. This permitted the goldsmith to check the registration and appearance of the parts to the whole during production. The soldered joints are skillfully chased, making the edges very difficult to discern on the outer surface. The edges, which run down from the shoulders on both sides of the statuette (fig. 41), are more readily apparent in the interior cavity.

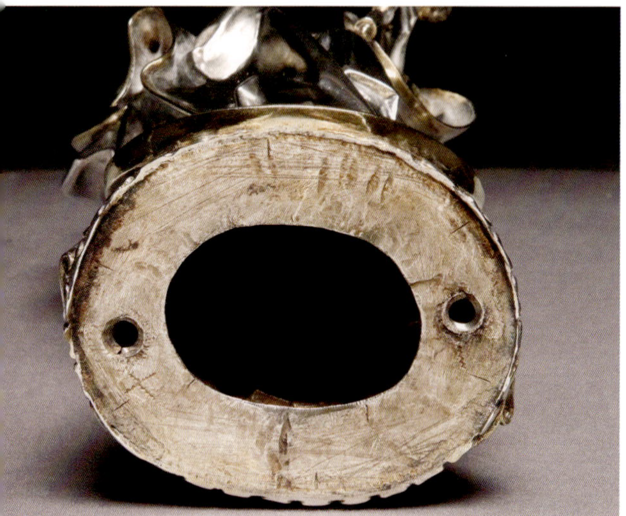

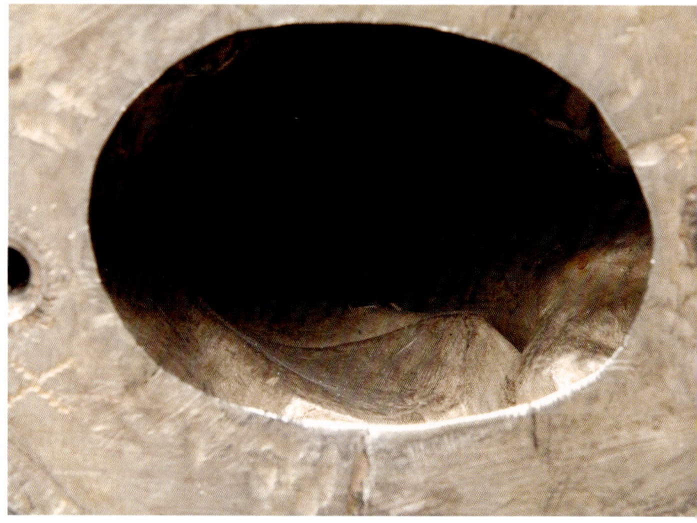

Figure 39. *The Kimbell Virgin and Child,* opening in the bottom of statuette

Figure 40. Interior cavity

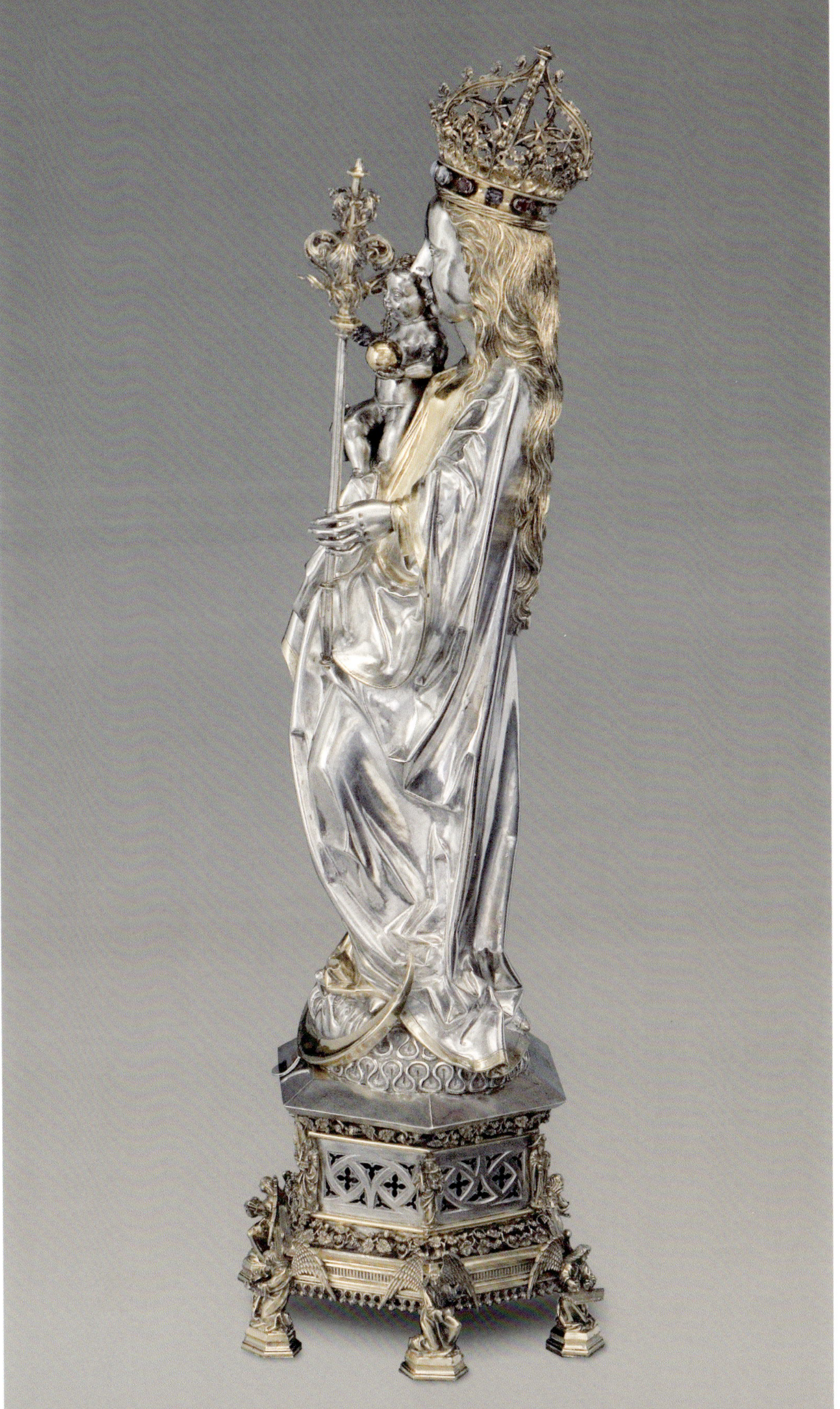

Figure 41.
View of the
right side

The metal sheets were worked using techniques known as embossing (or repoussé) and chasing. In the first, the forms are shaped by hammering from the reverse or inner side. Periodically the metal must be annealed or heated slightly to make it more malleable. This process tempers or strengthens the metal. A hole that has opened at the bottom of Mary's robe reveals the metal's thinness in certain passages. Chasing is used for working the metal from the exterior. A blunt tool known as a tracer (or ciselet) is hammered or pushed at an angle to the metal. This is especially evident in the compressed folds and sharp edges of the drapery. Engraving and chiseling added details to the surface. The artist made decorative features, such as the repetitive designs on the neckline of Mary's dress or the long parallel incisions of the trim of her robe, using a burin or another pointed tool like that employed by Saint Eligius's assistants (see fig. 32). Our goldsmith used a mix of these techniques to distinguish the individual strands of the Virgin's hair. A bit of punchwork, created when a punch bearing a specific decorative motif is hammered into the surface of the metal, is visible on the trim of Mary's sleeves and more clearly on the rear trim of her cloak.

The goldsmith cast the Virgin's hands separately. Her right hand slips into a tube with inset threading attached inside her cuff and secured by a screw. The left hand is placed within a threaded tube and pinned into position (fig. 42). The X-radiographs indicate that Christ's body is hollow but the fingers and toes are solid, suggesting it too was probably cast (fig. 43). Under close magnification,

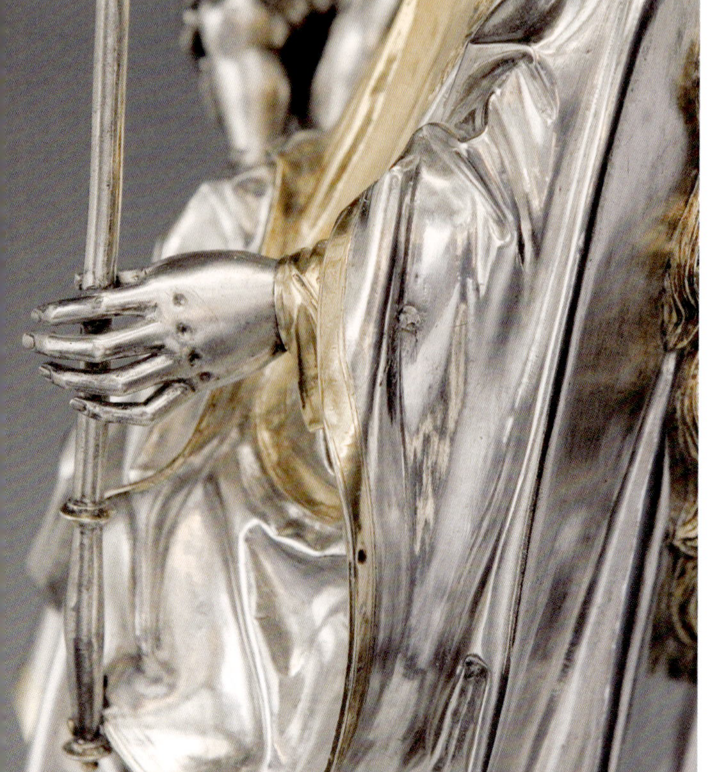

Figure 42. Virgin's left arm and hand with the joining pin (detail of fig. 41)

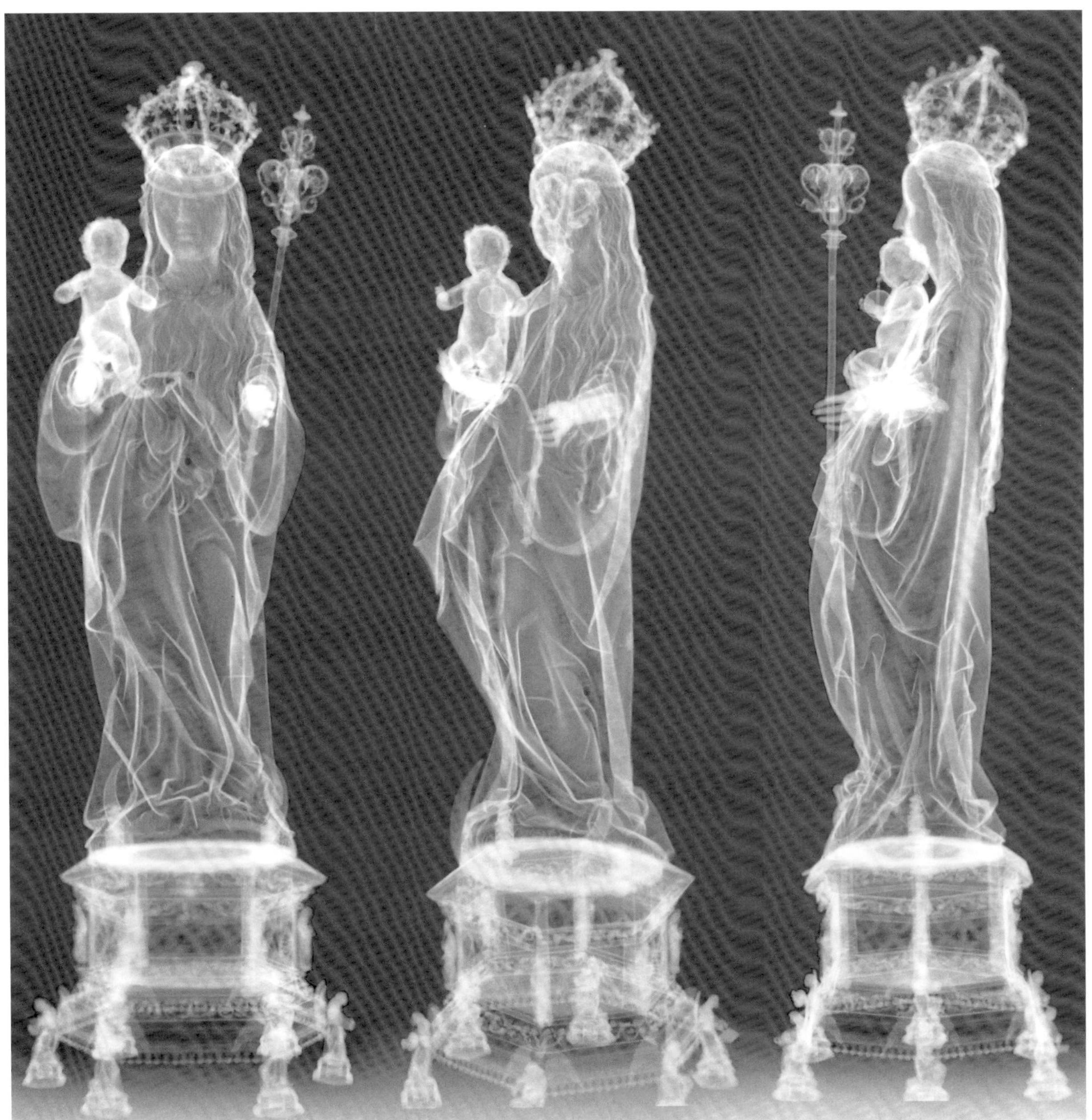

Figure 43. *The Kimbell Virgin and Child*, composite X-radiographs, 2003

Christ's face and body reveal tiny bubbles in the surface of the metal, another indication that the figure was likely cast rather than worked up from a sheet. Some engraving is evident in the strands of Christ's hair (fig. 44). He is supported solely by the solder joining his right leg to Mary's hand.

The remaining parts reveal a masterful mix of techniques. The Virgin's scepter is a hollow tube with knobs added to the shaft (fig. 45). The foliate decorations were cut from sheet silver and then shaped. Wires were soldered on to form the veins of the leaves. Mary's crown is more complex (see fig. 4). The fleurs-de-lis, the four supporting straps with leafy crockets, and, likely, the lost finial atop the crown are cast. The stars and joining wires are soldered to the straps. The band of the crown, formed from sheet silver, is edged with braided wire. The stones are placed in bezel, or beveled, settings and secured with silver posts soldered on the reverse side. The screw attaching the crown to

Figure 44. Christ Child's hair from the back

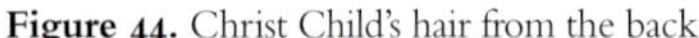

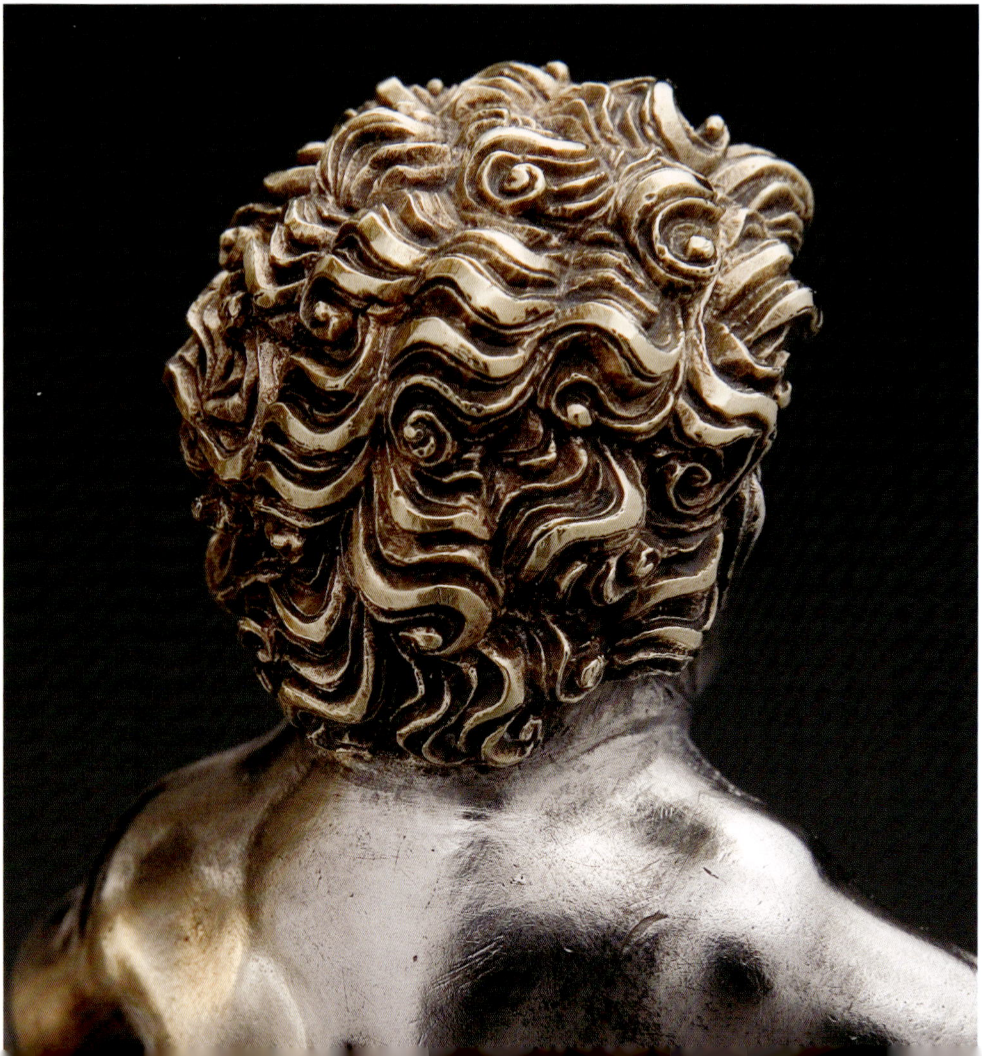

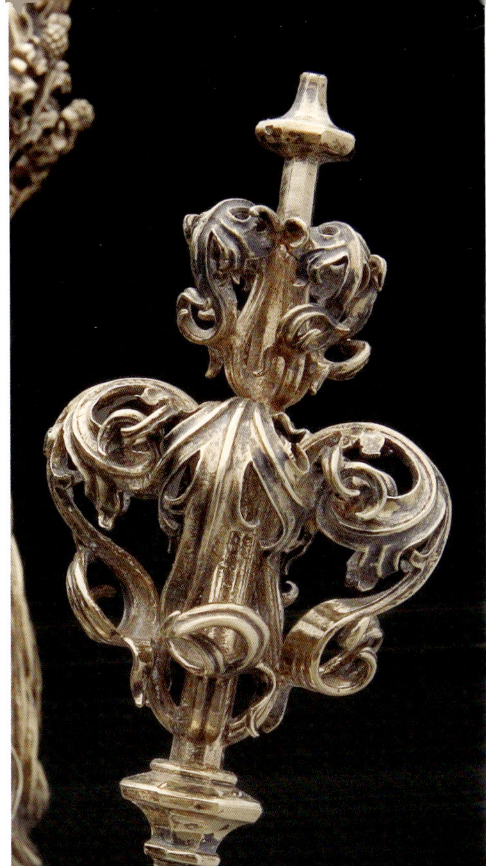

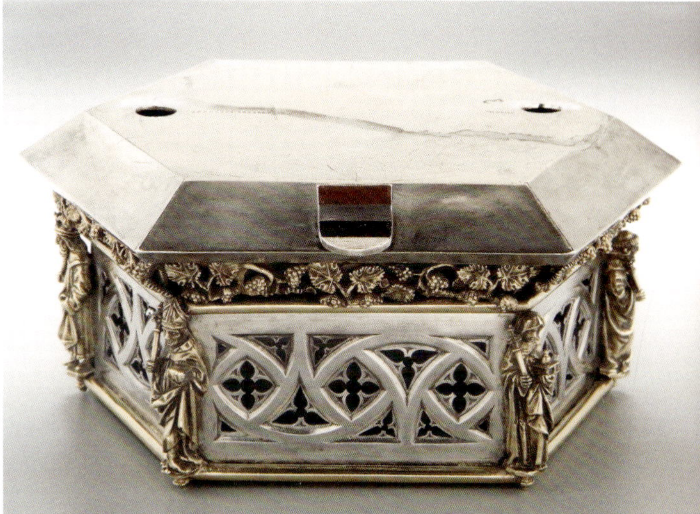

the Virgin's head is not original. The hexagonal plinth beneath Mary's feet and the base are formed from metal sheets, while the tiny angels and saints are cast (fig. 46; see fig. 15). The angels' instruments were only soldered on, which explains how two were lost.

The golden passages on the statuette are achieved using fire-gilt. Also known as mercury gilding, this technique involves dropping pieces of gold leaf or filings into boiling mercury. When cooled, this amalgam or paste is brushed on the parts to be gilded, such as the Virgin's dress and hair. The statuette is then heated, but not to the point that would melt or negatively affect the silver or the various soldered joints. This warming causes the mercury to evaporate and leaves behind a bonded layer of gold.

Finally, the surfaces are burnished or rubbed with an agate and then highly polished using a rabbit's foot (see fig. 32). With the passing of time, the silver and gilding have tarnished slightly.

One last feature needs explanation. On the back side of Mary, three holes have been drilled into her hair and another into the center of her cloak just below the knees (see fig. 5). The statuette was once fitted with a mandorla of sunrays, a common iconographic feature of the Virgin of the Apocalypse. These holes, crudely done, mar the respective surfaces. As Peter Dandridge has noted, "it would be the only instance where the goldsmith used screws without making use of sleeves with soldered-in threading." Otherwise, the craftsmanship of the *Kimbell Virgin and Child* is truly remarkable, and so, for aesthetic and technical reasons, I feel the statuette did not originally have a mandorla. Possibly the bishop's private altar included painted or gilded wooden rays before which the statuette could be placed (see fig. 64). It is unknown when the mandorla was added and then removed.

A Question of Origin

Where and by whom was the *Kimbell Virgin and Child* made? Around 1486, the leading south German goldsmith centers were Augsburg, Nuremberg, and Ulm. Further away one found concentrations of skilled goldsmiths in Basel, Cologne, Hamburg, Lübeck, Lüneburg, Breslau (Wrocław), and Dresden.[31] Most major towns possessed a few goldsmiths, so the artist or artists could have resided in Eichstätt or other nearby towns, such as Ingolstadt, Munich, Regensburg, or Würzburg. The pool of potential candidates shrinks, however, when a distinction is made between goldsmiths capable of producing statuettes versus those manufacturing utilitarian wares like bowls and cups or jewelry. The dearth of surviving statuettes exacerbates the problem of attribution. The names of hundreds of late fifteenth-century German goldsmiths are documented, but few can be linked with specific works. Whereas some objects bear punchmarks indicating artist and/or city, Marc Rosenberg's study of German goldsmith marks reveals these were not used systematically during the fifteenth and sixteenth centuries.[32] Ulm had a 1394 ordinance requiring stamping for works weighing over one half mark, yet none is recorded prior to the sixteenth century.[33] Augsburg's similar law dates only to 1529.[34] Nuremberg's ordinances required such marks, but it was not a common practice until after 1541.[35] The *Schlüsselfelder Ship* bears Nuremberg's city mark but not a master's symbol. No marks exist for Eichstätt until 1662.[36] Of the 4,443 objects in Fritz's corpus of late medieval goldsmith works from Central Europe, only 41 items were signed, and of these all but three date between 1450 and 1525.[37]

The record for south German goldsmiths authoring extant silver statuettes, as opposed to tiny figures, is even more woefully scant.[38] In 1472 Ingolstadt goldsmith Hans Greiff created a *Saint Anne Holding Mary and the Christ Child* (1472) for Anna Hofmann, the wife of the city's tax collector (fig. 47).[39] Presumably Frau Hofmann requested the inscription naming the artist, city, patron, and costs of materials and labor. In the 1480s Hufnagel of Augsburg and Balthasar Weltenperger of Passau fashioned attractive *Virgin and Childs* (see figs. 38, 55). Hans Müller and Jörg Seld of Augsburg as well as Paul Müllner (Möller) of Nuremberg are documented making statuettes, but do any survive (see fig. 54)?[40] The scarcity of names should be taken as a caution because we lack sufficient evidence to

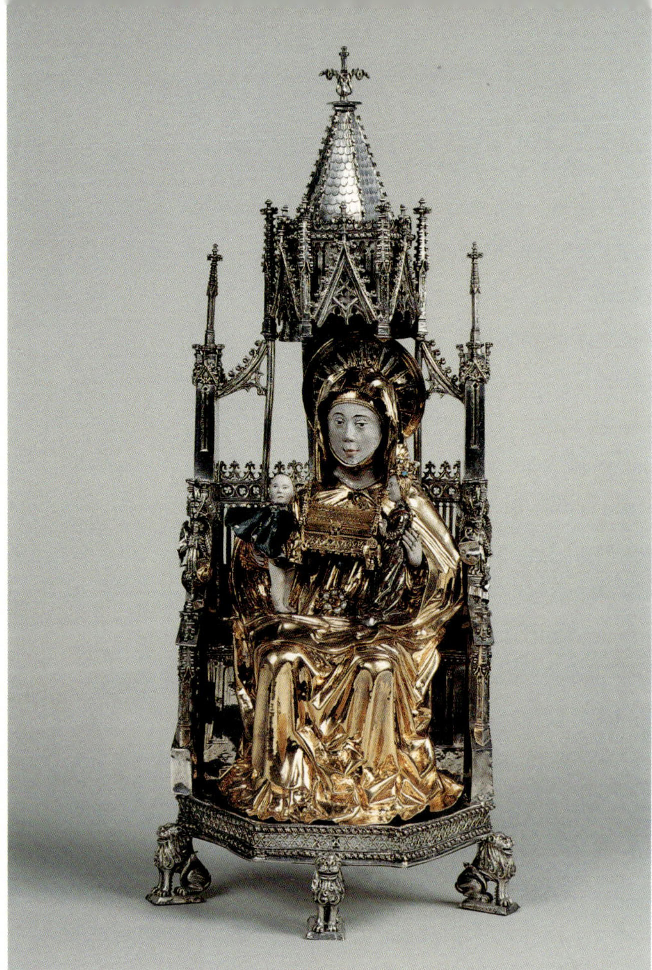

Figure 47. Hans Greiff, *Saint Anne Holding Mary and the Christ Child (Annaselbdritt)*, 1472. Silver with gilt and polychromy, 19⅛ x 8¼ in. (48.6 x 21 cm). Musée National du Moyen Age (Cluny), Paris (Cl. 3308)

make many definitive attributions. Between 1464 and 1496, the years of Bishop Wilhelm's reign, forty master goldsmiths in Ulm registered pupils.[41] Nuremberg had 140 goldsmiths listed between 1468 and 1518.[42] There are a few extant Nuremberg-made statuettes, though no goldsmith can be securely claimed as the author. Eichstätt's cathedral chapter paid Master Lorenz, a local goldsmith, for a bust of Saint Walburga in 1487.[43]

A search through the incomplete archival records of Bishop Wilhelm and the cathedral chapter, located mainly in Bayerisches Staatsarchiv in Nuremberg and the Diözesanarchiv in Eichstätt, failed to yield any documentation about the *Kimbell Virgin and Child*.[44] Therefore, let us consider stylistic characteristics as a means for determining its origins. In 1885 Ferdinand Luthmer localized it simply as south German.[45] A century later Dietmar Lüdke described it as Swabian (Augsburg?).[46] He found regional counterparts for the forms of the Virgin's head, eyes, and, more generally, the diagonal folds and drapery arrangement plus the type of Christ Child, noting the obvious similarities with Hufnagel's statuette (see fig. 38). In 2002, Norbert Jopek tentatively suggested an Ulm provenance. He wondered whether, like Hufnagel's *Virgin and Child*, the Kimbell statuette was based upon a wooden model carved by a sculptor in the Jörg Syrlin the Elder–Michel Erhart circle.[47] More recently, Jopek speculated that a Strasbourg sculptor, working in the naturalistic tradition of Nicolas Gerhaert, might have been contracted specially to make the model on which the silver statuette may have been based.[48]

As discussed, neither drawings nor a sculptural model are known for the *Kimbell Virgin and Child*. A standing Virgin carrying Christ was the most common subject in Late Gothic art. Crescent moons, scepters, crowns, and other details are mere adornments to the core image. Sometimes Mary holds Christ upright, as in our example, or she cradles his semireclining body. Most often, Christ rests on her left arm. Studying sculptural examples from Augsburg, Nuremberg, and Ulm, the leading centers near Eichstätt, one recognizes how quickly artistic ideas spread throughout the region. Artists, too, traveled between these towns. Thus it is possible to find individual features, such as the pose of the figures, the form of the tall crown, or the complicated drapery patterns, in a Madonna adorning a house façade or an altarpiece made in any of the three cities.[49] However, I have yet to find a sculpture that wholly reminds me of the Kimbell statuette. The mere resemblance of the eyes of one work, the dimples of another, the forehead type of a third are not, for me, compelling evidence of any direct association. When I viewed the *Kimbell Virgin and Child* in the 2002 Ulm sculpture exhibition, I was struck immediately by its lack of resemblance to the oeuvres of the Syrlins and Erharts. The marvelous balance of figures and the sophisticated handling of the details suggest that our unknown designer, whether a sculptor or a goldsmith, specialized in working on this scale rather than on larger statues.

Although the work may have been based on a model or drawing that originated in another city, the *Kimbell Virgin and Child* was probably made by an Augsburg goldsmith.[50] Dieter Lüdke's census lists seventy-one extant fifteenth- and early sixteenth-century German standing statuettes.[51] The composition of a Virgin and Child or of a saint standing on a multisided base was fairly standardized by 1486. The specifics of style and design reveal, however, that four of the five closest counterparts to the Kimbell statuette were created in Augsburg during the 1480s and 1490s. Hufnagel's *Virgin and Child* (1482) offers the best comparison (see fig. 38). Here Mary and her son stand on a hexagonal base carried by six music-playing angels. The sides are ornamented by five pairs of saints and, on the sixth side, a door to the relic compartment. The transition from the figure of the Virgin to the base is similar, if more abrupt, in the Berlin example, since it lacks the crescent moon and its plinth is thinner.

The scale and pose of the respective figures are quite alike. Yet there are significant aesthetic distinctions. Both goldsmiths combine silver and gilt; however, Hufnagel restricts the silver (now badly tarnished) to the flesh of his figures (fig. 48). As a result, his ensemble does not have the striking and subtly applied color contrasts of the Kimbell statuette, where Mary's golden hair plays against her silver cloak (figs. 49, 50). The Berlin Virgin is squatter and heavier looking than the more elongated

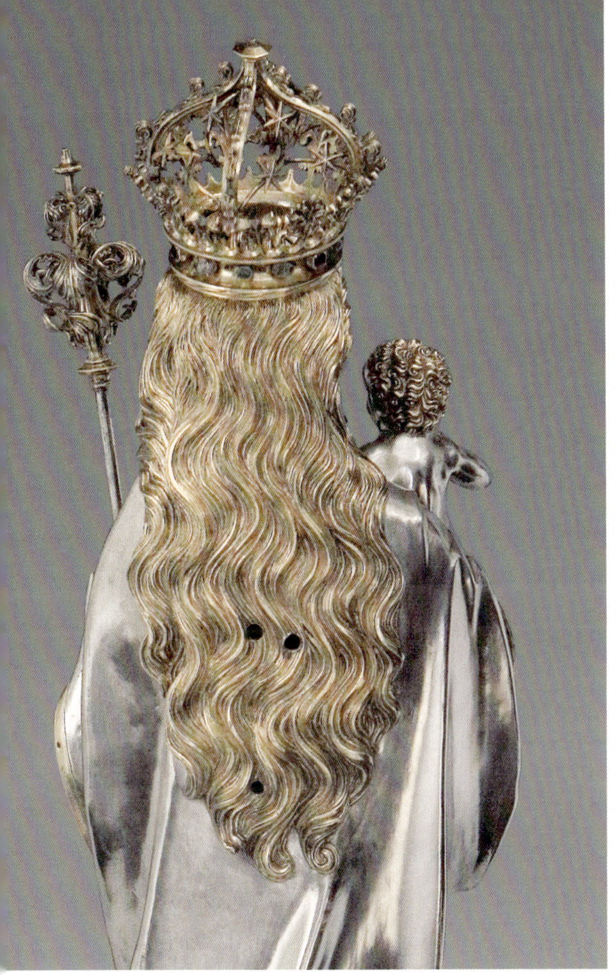

Figure 50. Upper half of Kimbell Virgin from the back

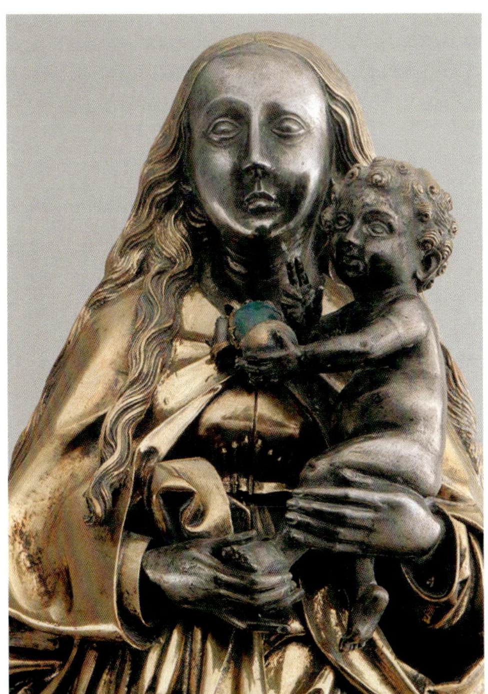

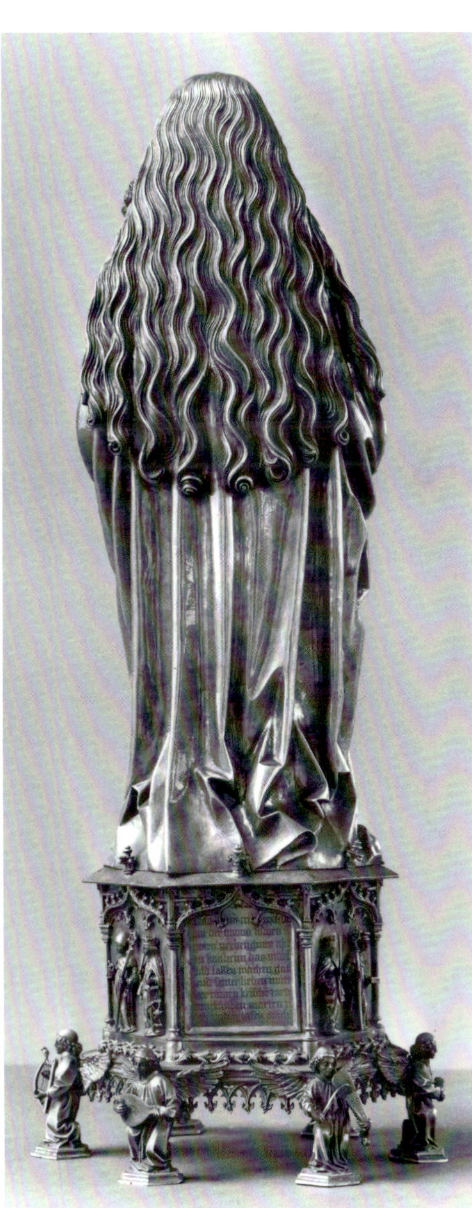

Figure 49. Heinrich Hufnagel, *Virgin and Child* (back side). See fig. 38

Figure 48. Heinrich Hufnagel, *Virgin and Child* (detail of fig. 38)

and more naturalistic Kimbell Virgin. The Berlin Mary's face is round, rather masklike, and lacks much individualization. Following his model, Hufnagel offers a compressed pose structured around the central vertical axis. His Virgin looks constrained by the weight of her robes in spite of the obvious attention to articulating the cloth. The Kimbell statuette's master devised a broader composition by placing Christ and the scepter away from the Virgin's body. This opens up the center of the ensemble so the viewer can admire the virtuosity of how the fabric around Mary's right arm dramatically billows out and down before exploding into the complex folds of the cloth gathered at her waist and the falling diagonals of the fabric.

I believe the Kimbell statuette follows the sorts of designs found just a few years earlier in Augsburg. Its goldsmith was more skilled than Hufnagel. Possibly Bishop Wilhelm could afford better artists or demand extra attention to details than Abbot Hans Fisches. Nevertheless, the commonalities of these two statuettes, I think, help localize the *Kimbell Virgin and Child* to Augsburg.

Another Augsburg goldsmith authored the silver *Virgin of the Apocalypse* formerly in the collegiate church of Saint Moritz in Augsburg (fig. 51).[52] This and a now-lost silver *Saint Michael* were given to the church probably around 1490 by Jacob Wirsung (Würsung), seal keeper and notary for the bishop of Augsburg. The height of the figure, 44.8 centimeters, is roughly the same as the Kimbell statuette minus its base. Here the Virgin looks down rather than out at the viewer, thus making the ensemble seem more intimate. The V-shaped treatment of the brow and nose recalls the Berlin statuette; however, this artist modeled his faces better than Hufnagel. The heavily faceted drapery animates the surface, though without the showy effects of the Berlin and Kimbell statuettes. In the nineteenth century, its base disappeared, and the silver on the back side of the Virgin was crudely cut out and removed.

The Cistercian abbey church at Kaisheim once possessed the Berlin *Virgin and Child* (1482), the London *Saint Sebastian* (1497), mentioned earlier, and the *Saint Christopher* (1493) in the collection of Kenneth Thomson (see figs. 36, 38, 52).[53] Made in Augsburg, these three goldsmith works fortunately survived the secularization of German monasteries and their holdings around 1803.[54] The two saints are posed more dramatically than the Virgin and Child statuettes. Christopher stares at the Christ Child with a mixture of surprise and awe as he struggles to carry him across the river. Sebastian's seemingly lifeless body slumps against the tree. The figure of Christopher is related loosely to the Basel drawing of the saint attributed to Jörg Schweiger, originally from Augsburg (see fig. 33). However, since Schweiger lived from about 1480 until 1534, this drawing must be based upon an older sketch, perhaps by someone in the circle of Hans Holbein the Elder. The designs for the two hexagonal bases of these saint statuettes skillfully mix small figures of saints or angels, foliate forms, and architectural elements, albeit in a different arrangement than the Virgin and Child statuettes.

The identities of the artist or artists of the two Kaisheim saints are unknown. Neither statuette is by Jörg Seld, Augsburg's leading goldsmith.[55] An independent master goldsmith from 1478 to 1527, his oeuvre ranged from elaborate tableware for the future emperor Maximilian I in 1491 to diverse religious objects for Augsburg's churches. For the local Benedictine monastery of Saints Ulrich and Afra, he devised a meter-tall monstrance-reliquary (1486–89) and a bust of Saint Narcissus worth

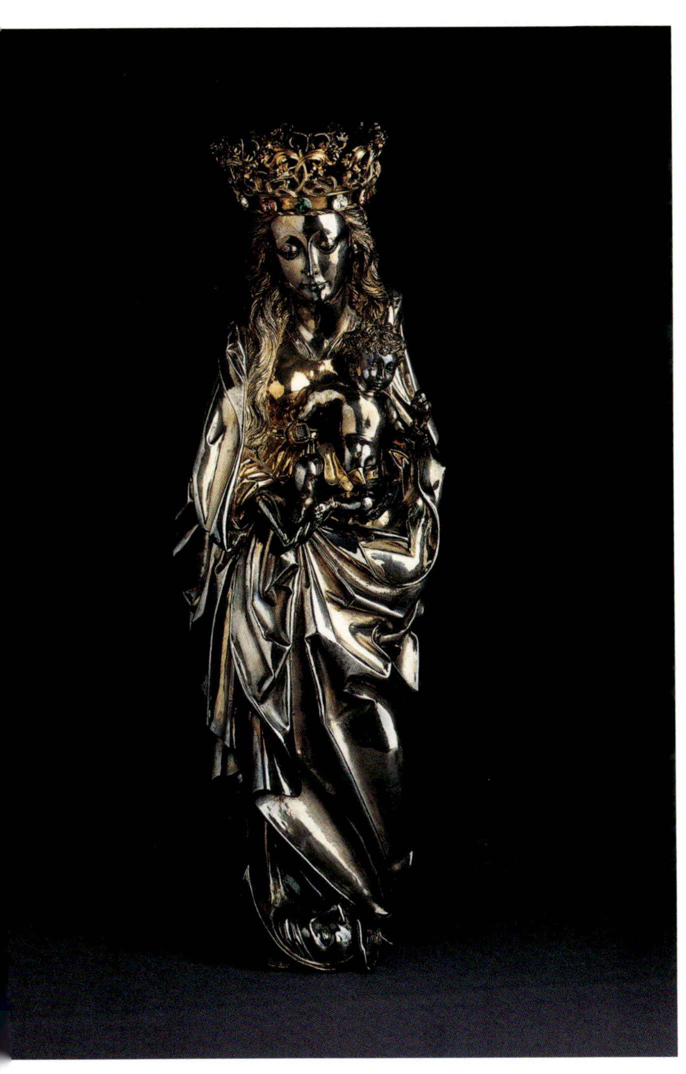

Figure 51. Augsburg goldsmith, *Virgin and Child of the Apocalypse*, c. 1490. Silver with gilt, 17⅞ x 6 in. (44.8 x 15.3 cm). Diözesanmuseum St. Afra, Augsburg (DMA 3039), on loan from the church of Saint Moritz, Augsburg

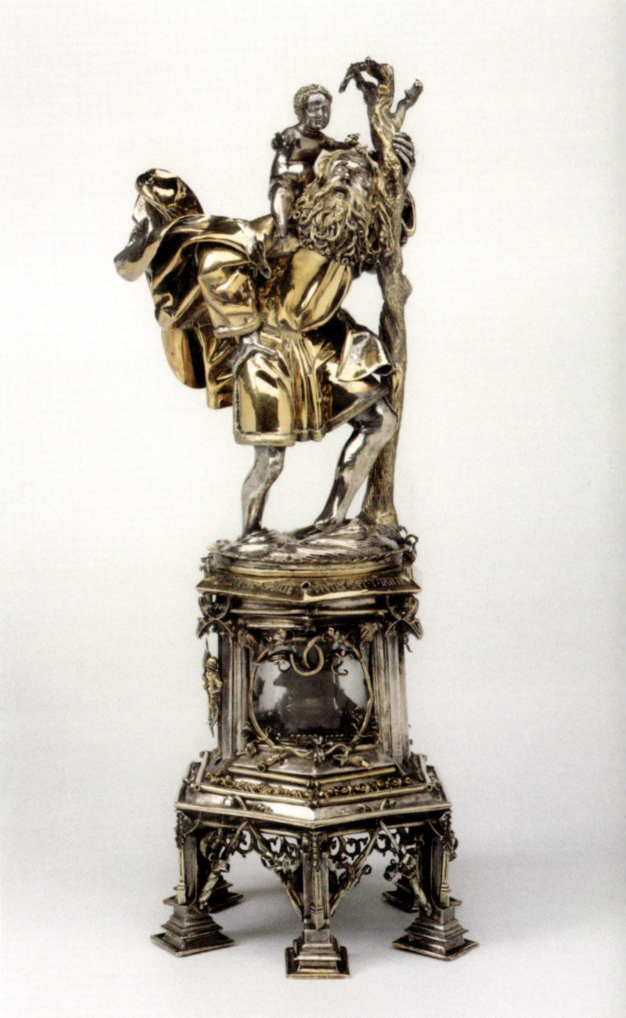

Figure 52. Augsburg goldsmith, *Saint Christopher*, 1493. Silver with gilt, height 18⅛ in. (46 cm). Kenneth Thomson Collection, Toronto

520 gulden.[56] For the cathedral, Seld produced a silver reliquary bust of Saint Simpert, weighing 48.4 pounds (22 kilos), and the *Silver Altar*, the former high altar measuring about 3.25 by 2.55 meters. This great retable, begun by goldsmith Peter Rempfing in 1482–86, was completed by Seld in 1506–9/10; Hans Holbein the Elder painted the wings.[57] Seld and Holbein's association began at least a decade earlier, in 1497, when the painter drew Seld's portrait.[58] They also collaborated on an altar (1502), now lost, for Saint Moritz's church. Seld's last known work was a seated silver *Virgin and Child* for the Kaisheim monastery, for which he was paid 500 gulden in 1519.[59]

The loss of Seld's larger figures deprives us of a proper basis for comparing his art with the *Kimbell Virgin and Child*. In 1492 Seld created the *Seld'sches Altärchen* (or *Little Eichstätt Altar*) for one of Bishop Wilhelm's closest advisors (fig. 53).[60] That summer Wilhelm sent Canons Bernhard and Konrad Adelmann von Adelmannsfelden of Eichstätt to England to deliver the relics of Saints Richard, Willibald, and Walburga to King Henry VII. To commemorate his safe return, Bernhard commissioned this silver altar using the 200 crowns the king had given him. Since an inscription praises the Virgin Mary, the altar is believed to have been presented to Unserer Lieben Frau, Eichstätt's collegiate parish church; however, as Peter Reindl has pointed out, the cathedral, which is dedicated to Mary, is an equally plausible setting.[61] The interior displays small figures of Saint Walburga in the center flanked by Saints Boniface and Richard on the left, and her two brothers Willibald and Wunibald on the right. The four engraved exterior scenes illustrate Willibald's life.

Did Bishop Wilhelm recommend Seld to his associate because he had employed him earlier? At the very least, Seld enjoyed a regional reputation by 1492. Canon Adelmann von Adelmannsfelden maintained close ties with the Swabian city, yet in the 1490s he was not the only prominent Eichstätt cleric to patronize Augsburg's artists.[62] When ordering Wilhelm's tomb and the commemorative miniature in the *Pontifikale Gundekarianum*, Gabriel von Eyb, his successor, looked first to Augsburg (see figs. 64, 68). Similarly, Holbein and Augsburg painter-glazer Gumpold Giltlinger created the attractive *Last Judgment* window (c. 1502) in the Mortuarium of Eichstätt Cathedral (see fig. 71), and Holbein's design for another window depicting Saints Willibald, Richard, Wunibald, and Walburga is today in Basel.[63] A decade later sculptor Loy Hering, Eichstätt's greatest Renaissance artist, moved there from Augsburg. Even though these examples postdate 1486, Eichstätt historically first turned to Augsburg and second to Nuremberg for its artists. I have not found any relevant link with Ulm's artistic community. There was considerable interaction between the bishops of Eichstätt and Augsburg, whose dioceses bordered each other, resulting in initiatives such as the joint founding of the University of Ingolstadt in 1472, and both dioceses fell under the jurisdiction of the archbishop of Mainz.

The stylistic affinities of the *Kimbell Virgin and Child* with works by Augsburg's goldsmiths are stronger than any other alternative. For every good hypothesis, however, there is a caveat. High-quality silver statuettes were popular throughout this period, and much of our evidence remains lost. Lucas Cranach the Elder's *Wittenberger Heiltumsbuch* (1509) illustrates the famous collection of 5,005 relics amassed by Friedrich the Wise, elector of Saxony.[64] Included among the 123 woodcuts are 27 male and 8 female silver statuettes. His *Virgin and Child* contained over four dozen holy remains associated with Mary (fig. 54).[65] Although many of Friedrich's reliquaries were made in Leipzig and other Saxon towns, he commissioned goldsmiths in Augsburg, Nuremberg, as in this case, and a host of other locales. The small town of Kösslarn, a regional pilgrimage site dedicated to the Virgin Mary in eastern

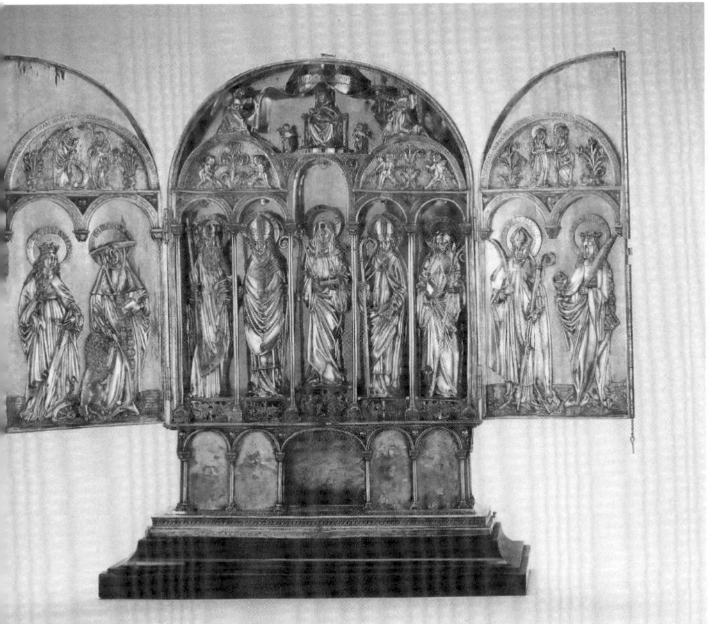

Figure 53. Jörg Seld, *Seld'sches Altärschen [Little Eichstätt Altar]*, 1492. Silver with gilt; open without socle: 18⁷⁄₁₆ x 24¹⁵⁄₁₆ in. (46.8 x 63.3 cm). Wittelsbacher Ausgleichsfonds, Munich (S I 12)

Der Sybent gang

Zum .v. Ein silbern
Bildt der Jungkfrawen Marie
Von der Stat do die Jungkfraw
Maria geborn ist ein partickel
Von etlichen seden die sye gespun-
nen hatt ein partickel
Vom hauß doryn sie gewont als
sy vierzehen Jar alt gewest .j. ptic.
Von der stat des bergs Syon vnd
dem Maria gewont hat .ij. ptick.
Von der Kamern do Maria von
dem Engel gegrust wart .ij. ptic.
Von der Millich der Jungkfraw
Marie .v. partickel
Von dem Baum do Maria den
herren gesauget hat bey dem Bal-
sam garten ein partickel
Von den haren Marie .iiij. ptickel
Von dem hembdt Marie .ij. ptic.
Vom Rock Marie drey ptickel
Von andern kleydern Marie .viij.
partickel
Von der gurtel Marie vier ptickel
Von den schlayren Marie vij. pti.
Vom schlayr marie besprengt mit
dem Blut Cristi vnd dem Creutze
zwey partickel
Von der stat do Maria gestorben
ist ein partickel
Vom wachs des liechts das vnser frawen in die hant gegeben / als sye
gestorben ist ein partickel
Vom wachs das Maria einer andechtigen Matron gegeßen .j. ptickel
Vom grabe marie .vj. ptic. Von d erden auß dem grabe marie ij. pti.
Von der stat do die Jungkfraw Maria zu hymel genumen ist .j. ptic.
Summa .lvj. partickel

Figure 54. Paul Müllner (Möller), *Virgin and Child*, silver reliquary (now lost) made for the palace church in Wittenberg, 1501–2. Woodcut illustration in Lucas Cranach the Elder, *Wittenberger Heiltumsbuch* (Wittenberg, 1509), Gang no. 7, Reliquiar no. 5. Bayerische Staatsbibliothek, Munich

Bavaria, still possesses the silver *Virgin and Child* (1485/86–88) ordered from Balthasar Weltenperger, a goldsmith in nearby Passau (fig. 55).[66] Although the Virgin looks down, there are a lot of similarities with the Kimbell statuette. She holds her son and a flowering scepter, and her crown incorporates twelve stones set between two horizontal bands of twisted wire. Even the form of the crescent moon, which was likely cast separately and attached to the accompanying face, recalls that of the Kimbell

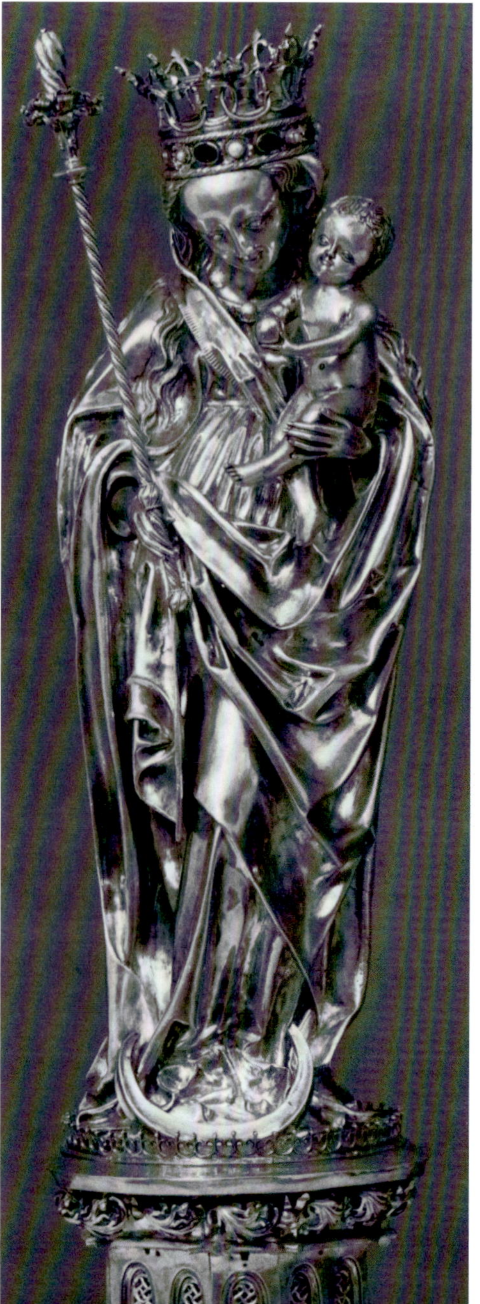

Figure 55. Balthasar Weltenperger, *Virgin of the Apocalypse*, 1485/86–88. Silver with gilt, 34¼ in. (87 cm). Katholisches Pfarrkirchenstiftung, Kösslarn

Figure 56. Wilhelm von Reichenau and Saint William of Maleval, from the tomb of Wilhelm von Reichenau (detail of fig. 68), before 1500. Willibald's choir, Eichstätt Cathedral

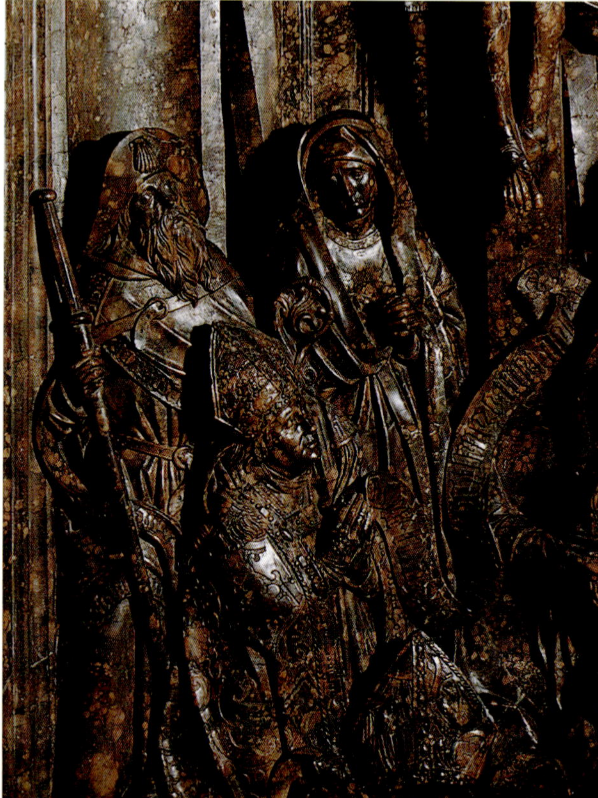

statuette. Impressive too are the deep, clearly articulated drapery folds and touching gesture of Christ as he holds the orb as if offering it to the viewer and, unconsciously, crosses one leg over the other. Still, Weltenperger's figures, measuring almost twice the size of the Kimbell statuette, are rather stylized and lack the surface articulation that distinguishes the smaller work.

Bishop Wilhelm von Reichenau and Eichstätt

Wilhelm von Reichenau, prince-bishop of Eichstätt, typifies a class of powerful patrons who are largely unknown today because many of their artistic commissions have disappeared and their building efforts obliterated by war or changing tastes. Born in about 1426 in Schloss Burgriesbach near Berching, Wilhelm belonged to a Franconian noble family (fig. 56).[67] He studied in Eichstätt's cathedral school and at the University of Erfurt in 1445 before going to Padua in 1458 to complete his education. Wilhelm returned soon, since Bishop Johann von Eich of Eichstätt appointed him cathedral canon. He was named general vicar of the diocese in 1459 and cathedral provost in 1461. During von Eich's illness, from 1461 to 1464, Wilhelm ably administered the diocese and Hochstift (principality). Then and especially during his own reign, he strengthened the bishop's political authority, improved the finances of the Hochstift, and expanded its borders through the strategic purchasing of villages and estates.

Contemporaries described Wilhelm as a tall, lean man who was wise and "dressed in all virtues."[68] His reign fell between those of von Eich, a staunch reformer, and Gabriel von Eyb (r. 1496–1535), a noted humanist. Wilhelm continued reforming the clergy. In 1480 he ordered a General Visitation of the diocese's roughly 120 parishes and 300 filial churches.[69] The report resulted in a synod in 1484, new statutes and standards for clergy, and common liturgical texts. Wilhelm recruited Georg Reiser (Reyser), who set up Eichstätt's first printing press in 1479.[70] Reiser published mainly texts for the bishopric including Eichstätt's *Breviary* (1483), three editions of missals (1486, 1489, 1494) with the arms of the bishop and cathedral chapter, a collection of synodal statutes (1484), and the *Obsequiale*, or *Rituale*, of the diocese (1486, 1488). Wilhelm's diplomatic skills, especially in mediating political disputes, earned the bishop the nickname "Friedenmacher" (Peacemaker).[71] In 1487 he brokered an accord between Emperor Friedrich III (r. 1440–93) and Duke Albrecht IV of Bavaria (r. 1465–1508). At the emperor's funeral in Vienna in 1493, Maximilian I (r. 1493–1519), his heir, referred to the bishop as "his father."

Wilhelm founded several institutions. He was the inaugural chancellor of the University of Ingolstadt, which was conceived already in 1465 but formally opened on June 26, 1472, with 489 enrolled students.[72] Aided by the bishop of Augsburg, Wilhelm's objective was to have a regional university so the students would not have to go abroad for their education. In 1469–71, Wilhelm helped establish the Augustinerinnenkloster Marienstein.[73] Although much of the convent was burned in 1634 by Landgrave Johann von Hessen and the Swedes, a stone tablet with Wilhelm's coat of arms and the painted date 1487 survives. Between 1482 and 1488, he sponsored the building of Marienburg, another Augustinian convent in Abenberg (fig. 57).[74]

The bishop is best remembered for his architectural patronage.[75] Eichstätt Cathedral was reconstructed between 1348 to 1363, when the eastern choir was built, and 1396, when the hall-style nave and aisles were finished (figs. 58, 59).[76] Wilhelm added the complex's remaining structures. As provost

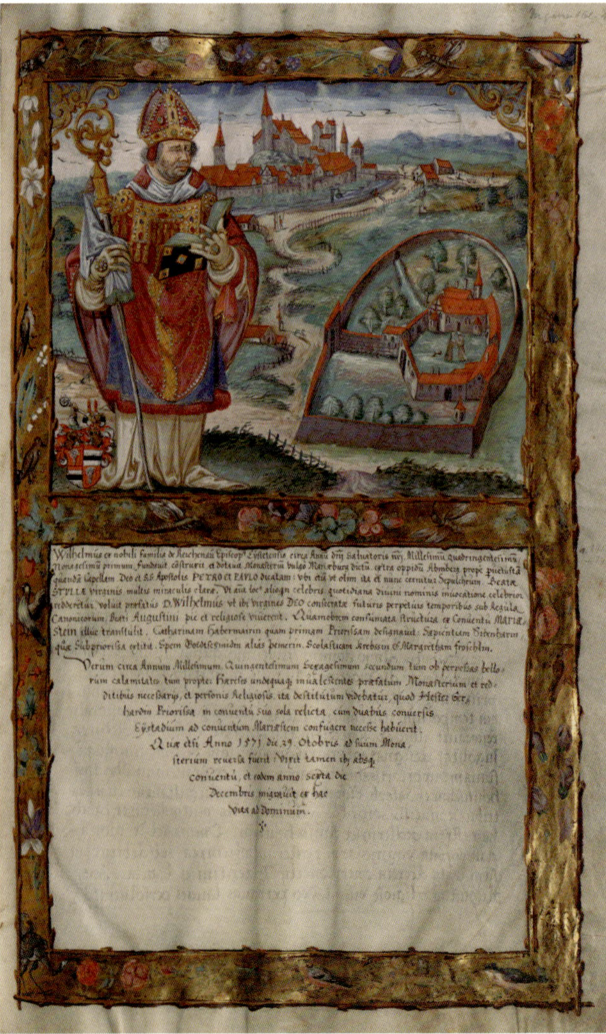

Figure 57. Wilhelm von Reichenau standing beside Marienburg convent at Abenberg, c. 1588. Miniature bound in *Missale secundum Chorum et Ritum Eystetensis Ecclesie*, 1517. Bayerische Staatsbibliothek, Munich (Rar 142, fol. 1 recto)

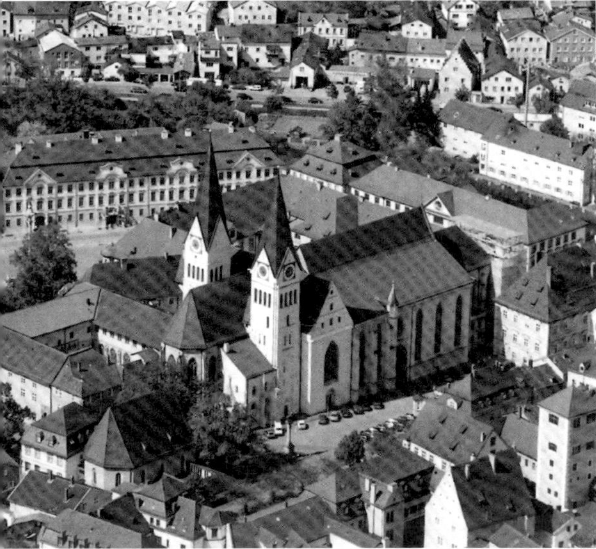

Figure 58. Eichstätt Cathedral and Bishop's Palace

Figure 59. Plan of Eichstätt Cathedral
1 Church
2 Cloister
3 Mortuarium
   A Beautiful Column
   B Epitaph of Wilhelm von Reichenau and his family
   C *Last Judgment* window
   D *Schutzmantel* window
   E Keystone with Wilhelm von Reichenau's coat of arms
4 Bishop's Palace
5 Willibald's choir with western bay extension
   A Shrine of Saint Willibald
   B Tomb of Wilhelm von Reichenau
   C Western bay with gallery and altar
6 Choir
   A Altar of the Virgin (High Altar)
7 Sacristy

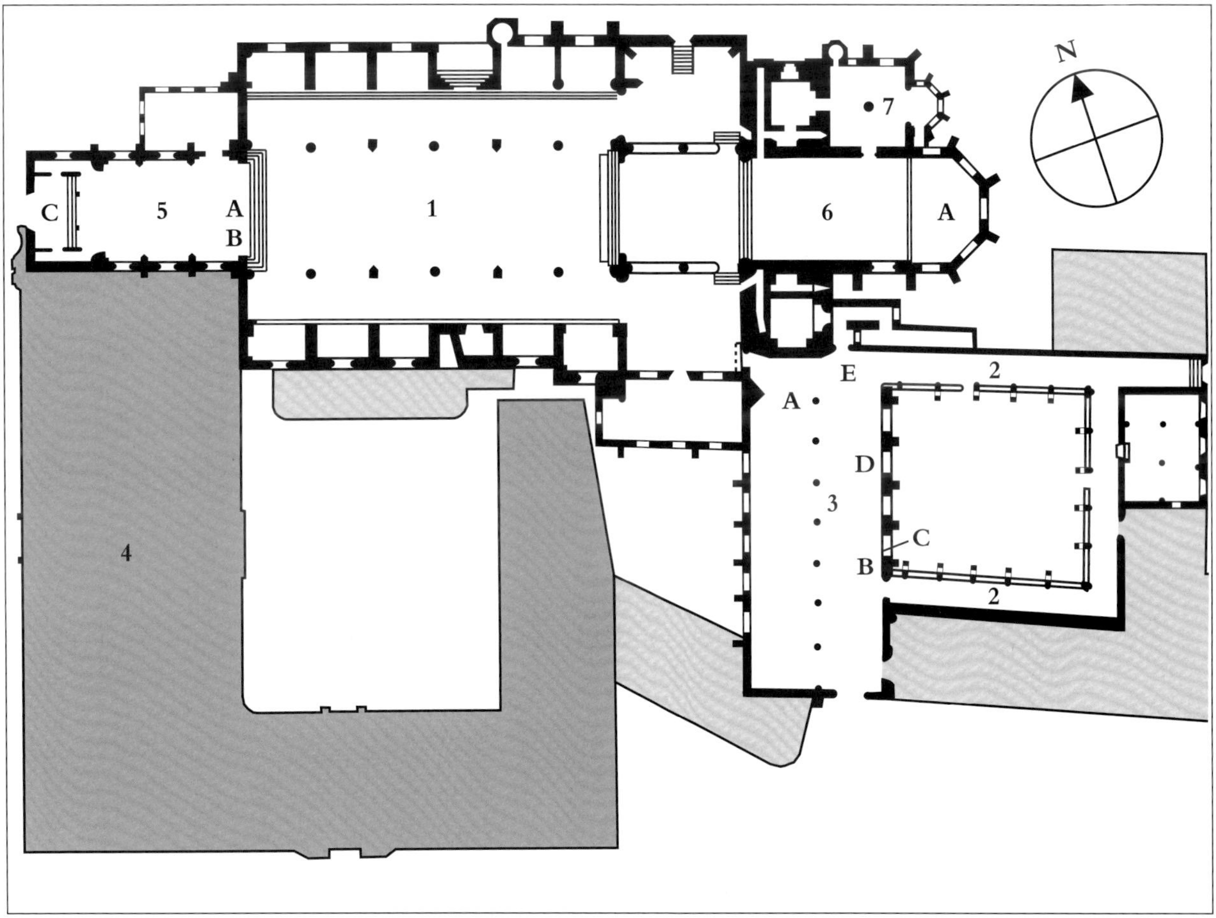

for von Eich, he and the cathedral chapter erected a new sacristy (1463/64, with the vaults dated 1480) (see fig. 73).[77] In 1471 he expanded the small Willibald's, or western, choir, the site of the shrine of Saint Willibald, by adding a deep fourth bay ornamented with rustic branchlike ribs (fig. 60).[78] This bay included an elevated gallery where Wilhelm placed his personal altar dedicated to the Holy Cross.[79] The gallery served as his private passage joining the church with the adjacent Alter Hof, the two-story episcopal residence and administrative building, which Wilhelm rebuilt at great expense (see fig. 25).[80]

Figure 60. Willibald's choir, with western bay extension, completed 1471. Eichstätt Cathedral

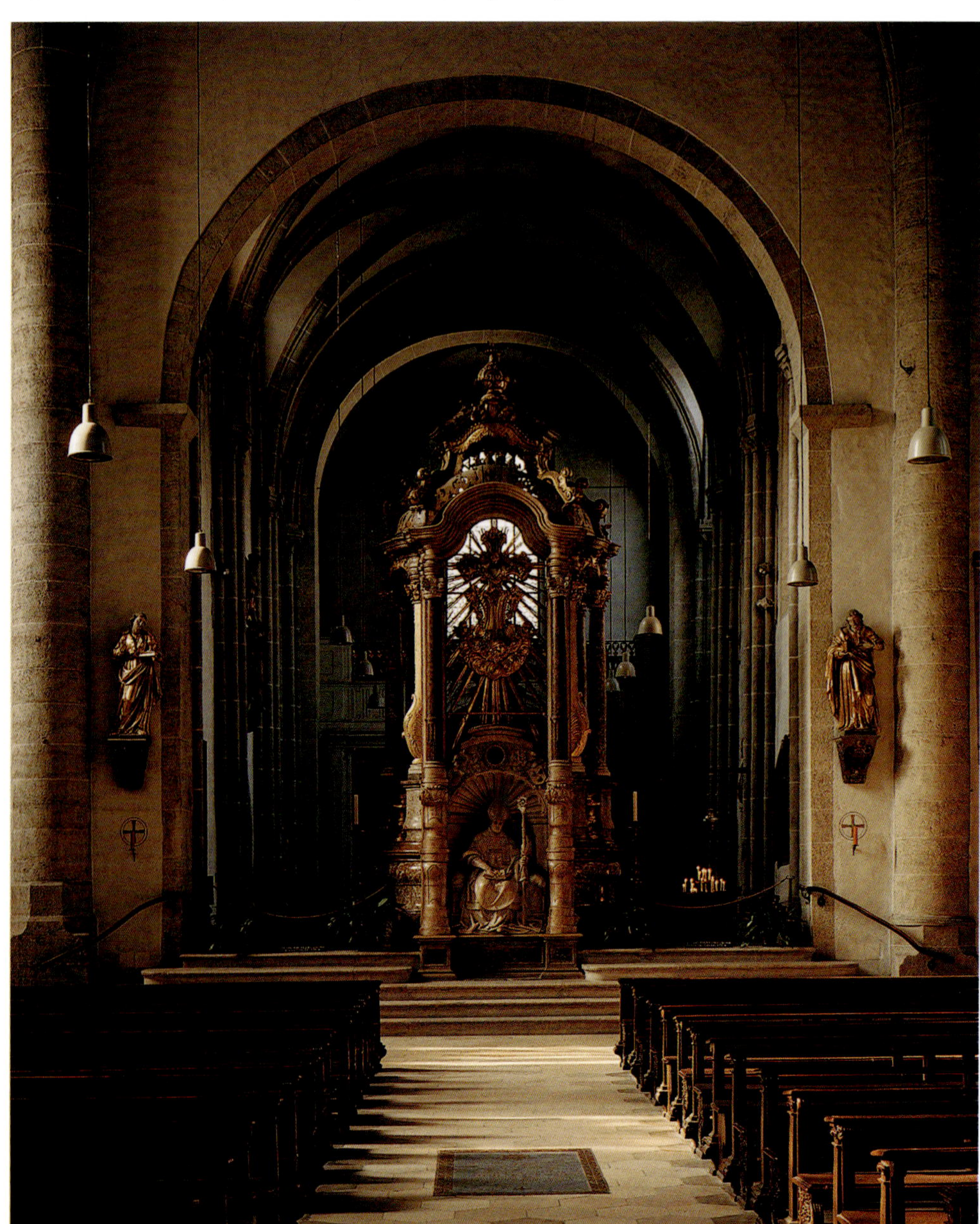

This included a huge great hall with an attractive wooden ceiling, according to the Augsburg art dealer Philipp Hainhofer, who saw it before the Swedish-led troops razed the palace on December 7, 1633.

Wilhelm's most impressive surviving project is the cathedral cloister. During the 1460s, he oversaw the construction of the east and south wings; the north wing dates to the 1410s. Wilhelm's arms adorn one of the east-wing keystones. The Mortuarium (c. 1480–1504), or west side, is a masterpiece of Late-Gothic German architecture (fig. 61).[81] Among other uses, the cathedral canons were buried

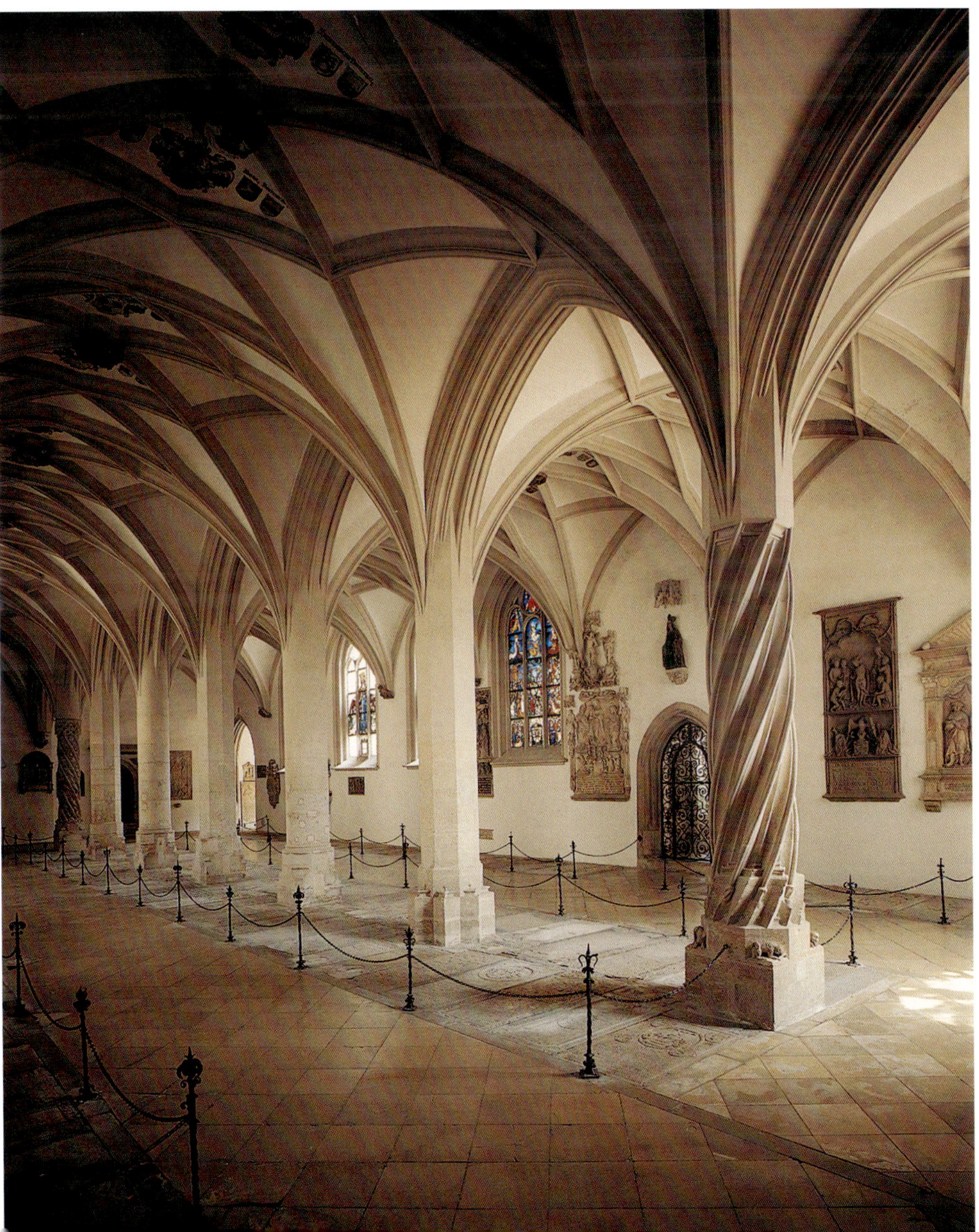

Figure 61. Attributed to Hans Paur, Mortuarium, c. 1480–1504. Hall measures 113 x 44 x 25 ft. (34.3 x 13.3 x 7.65 m). Eichstätt Cathedral

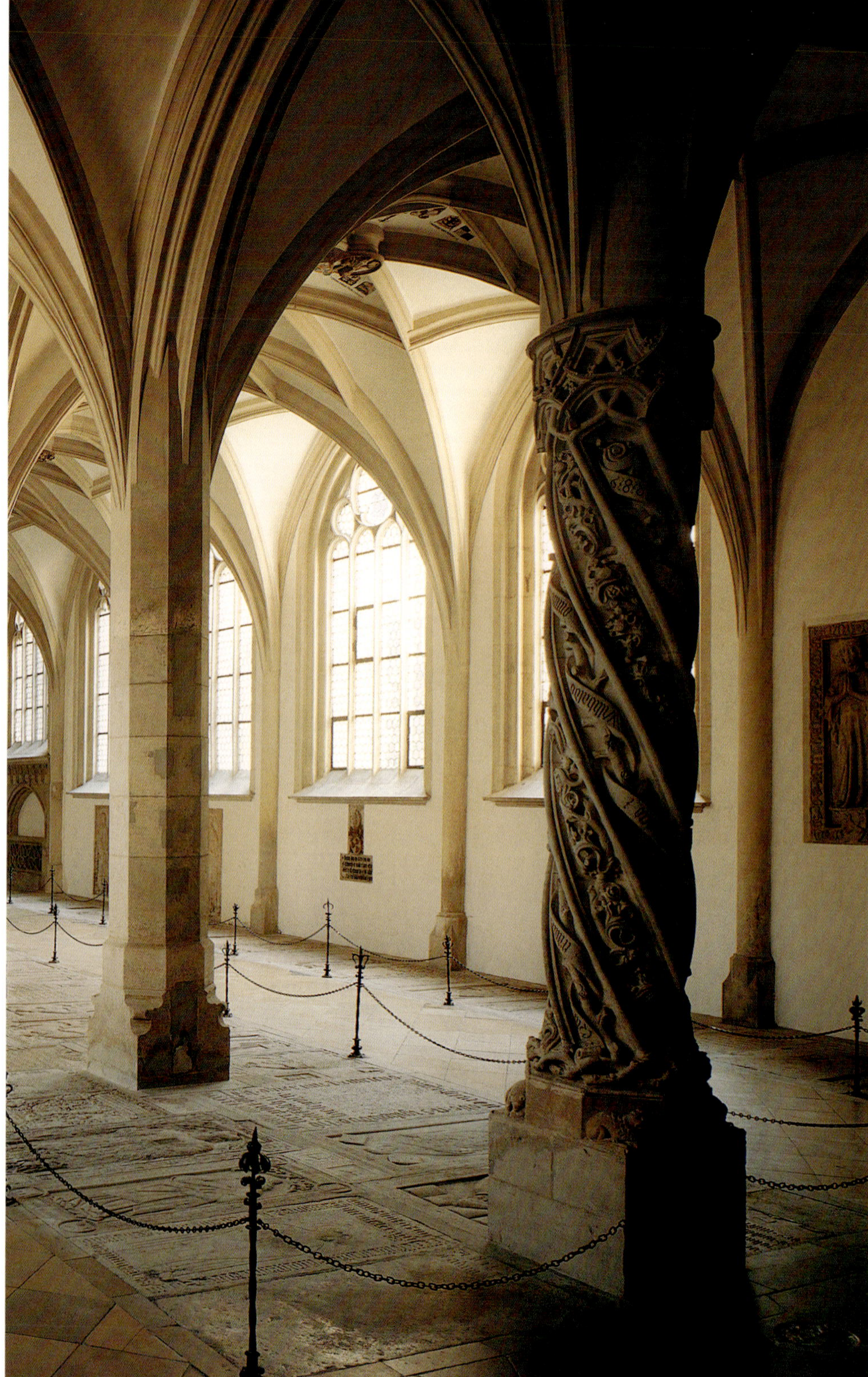

Figure 62. Attributed to Hans Paur, *Beautiful Column*, Mortuarium, inscribed 1489. Eichstätt Cathedral

in this two-aisled hall. Masses for their souls once were recited daily at four altars here. The Beautiful Column (*schöne Säule*), closest to the church, bears a prominent Latin inscription between its twisted ribs (fig. 62). It reads, "In my [Wilhelm's] presence was the construction in 1489 consecrated to the Virgin Mary, Saint Willibald, and all souls. Whoever passes by here may pray for the souls that rest in peace."[82] The architect was likely Hans Paur, the *thummaister* (cathedral master) from at least 1486 to 1508, who is probably portrayed in the bust on the north wall.[83] The Mortuarium still retains some of its original stained-glass windows and epitaphs, including Wilhelm's (see figs. 66, 71, 72).

During the 1470s, Wilhelm employed Mathes Roriczer (Roritzer), a member of a distinguished family of architects. Conrad, his father, was the master of Regensburg Cathedral, a post that Mathes assumed in 1478. Hans Paur was his uncle. In 1486 Roriczer dedicated his *Das Büchlein von der Fialen Gerechtigkeit* (*Booklet Concerning Pinnacle Correctitude*), a text on the proper use of geometry in architecture, to Bishop Wilhelm.[84] The first published German architecture treatise, it opens with Wilhelm's coat of arms and a flowery laudation praising his support of the project (fig. 63).

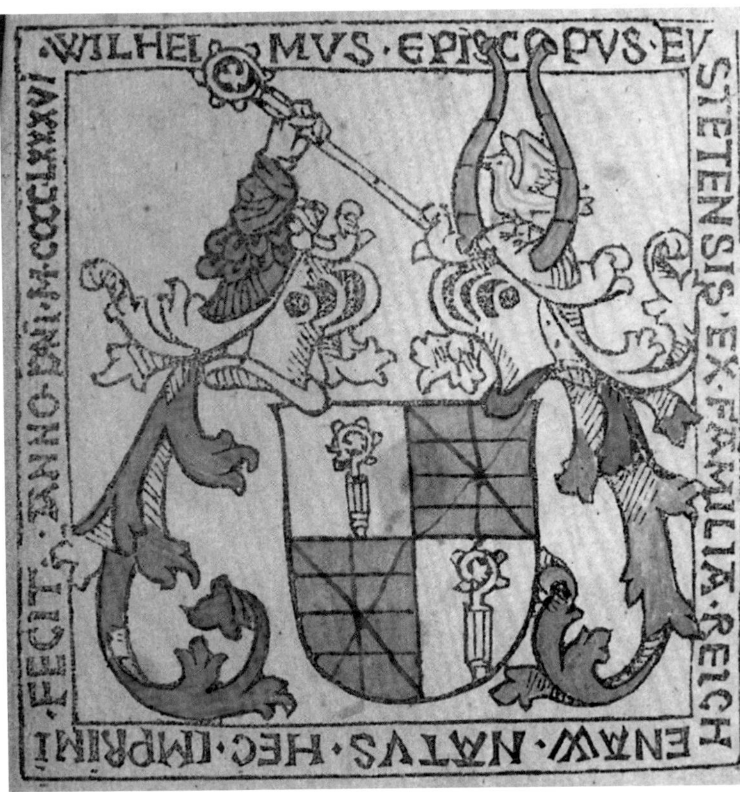

Figure 63. Mathes Roriczer, *Das Büchlein von der Fialen Gerechtigkeit [Booklet Concerning Pinnacle Correctitude].* Regensburg, 1486, fol. 2 verso, 7½ x 5⅜ in. (19.1 x 13.7 cm). Staatliche Bibliothek, Regensburg (Sign.: IM/4Inc.238)

Wilhelm von Reichenau venerated the Virgin Mary. The *Pontifikale Gundekarianum*, an invaluable source, includes biographies of Eichstätt's bishops from Gundekar II the Pious (r. 1057–75) to Moritz von Hutten in the mid-sixteenth century.[85] Wilhelm's biography, written by Leonhard Angermaier, his personal chaplain, recounts his devotion to Mary. Besides establishing two convents in her honor, Wilhelm instituted the Feast of the Presentation in the Temple of the Blessed Virgin Mary on November 21 in the cathedral and diocese liturgical calendars in 1488.[86] Angermaier next remarks

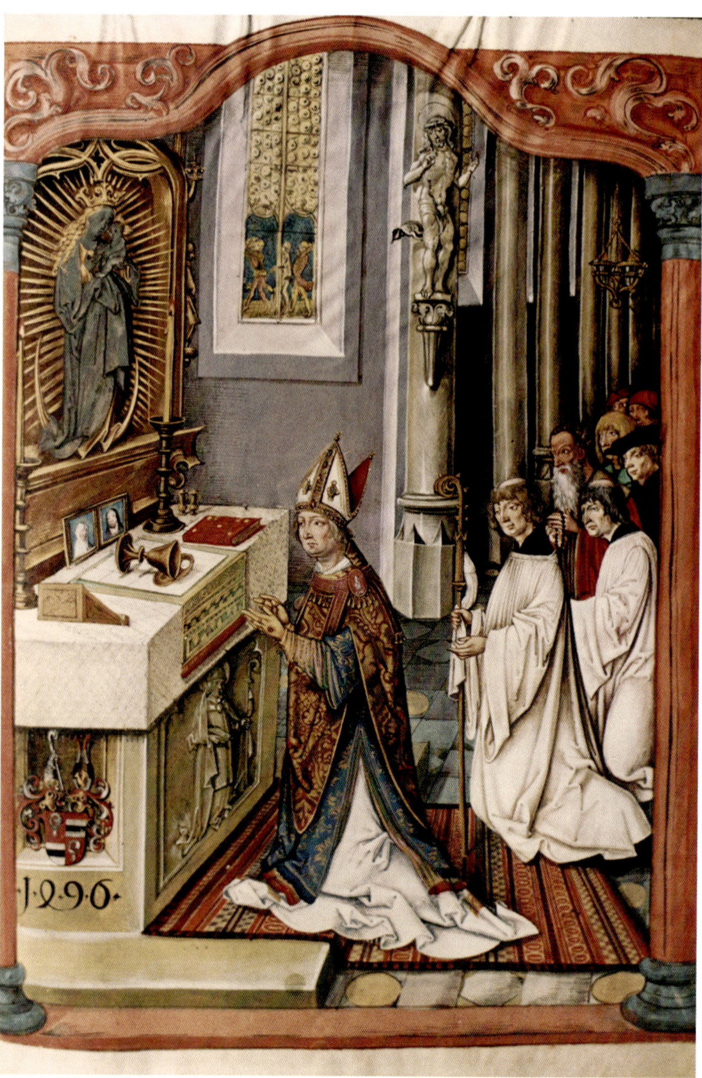

Figure 64. Augsburg Illuminator, *Wilhelm von Reichenau at Mass*, from the *Pontifikale Gundekarianum*, c. 1501–2. Miniature, 16⅛ x 12³⁄₁₆ in. (41 x 31 cm). Diözesanarchiv Ordinariatsbibliothek, Eichstätt (MS Codex B4, folio 41 recto)

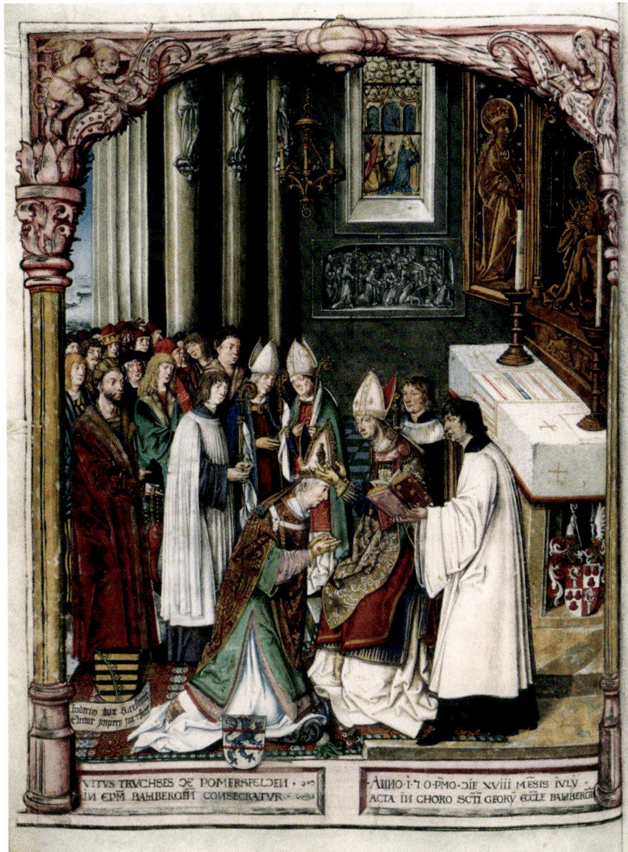

Figure 65. Augsburg Illuminator, *Gabriel von Eyb, Bishop of Eichstätt, Consecrating Veit Truchsess von Pommersfelden, Bishop of Bamberg (r. 1501–3), in Bamberg Cathedral.* From the *Pontifikale Gundekarianum,* c. 1501–2. Miniature, 16⅛ x 12³⁄₁₆ in. (41 x 31 cm). Diözesanarchiv Ordinariatsbibliothek, Eichstätt (MS Codex B4, folio 43 verso)

that Wilhelm "caused a silver image of the Blessed Virgin Mary to be made and gave it to the cathedral church" (Imaginem argenteam beate Marie Virginis fieri fecit, et ecclesie cathedrali donauit). This silver image is certainly the *Kimbell Virgin and Child.*

A stylized portrait of Wilhelm commissioned by Gabriel von Eyb, his successor, accompanies the biography (fig. 64). The anonymous Augsburg illuminator shows Wilhelm kneeling quietly in prayer before an altar.[87] The mensa is adorned with Wilhelm's coat of arms, the date 1496, a carved or woven altar frontal depicting Saint Willibald, and a small painted diptych of the Virgin and Christ. Behind the altar stands a large Virgin of the Apocalypse set in a wooden frame before a painted mandorla of rays. The Flagellation of Christ in stained glass and a sculpted Man of Sorrows decorate the adjacent wall. Wilhelm is joined by seven men, possibly including Angermaier holding the bishop's crozier.

The scene is fictitious, yet it represents two important points. First, I think that this Marian statue is intended to be the *Kimbell Virgin and Child,* an object that the illuminator had never personally seen but was instructed to represent. As a result, it is painted much too large and slightly different in composition. The same illuminator portrayed von Eyb attending the consecration of Veit Truchsess von Pommersfelden, bishop of Bamberg (r. 1501–3) in Bamberg Cathedral (fig. 65). Here the altarpiece is clearly made of polychromed wood, while Wilhelm's statue is silver with partial gilt. He accurately dressed both Eichstätt bishops in the new rational, a decorative liturgical vestment worn over the shoulders.[88]

The statuette must have been of exceptional importance to Wilhelm to be mentioned in this vita, which is filled with deeds and not references to works of art; Angermaier and von Eyb, among the bishop's closest advisors, knew this. Wilhelm used this portable statuette for his private devotions. At different times, it may have been placed in the bishop's chapel in the Alter Hof, on his personal altar in the Willibald's choir gallery, perhaps on one of the cathedral's altars, and possibly even was carried in religious processions. The *Kimbell Virgin and Child*'s iconography is uniquely suited to Eichstätt, as Wilhelm sought intercession and protection for the diocese from the Virgin and Saints Richard, Willibald, Wunibald, and Walburga.

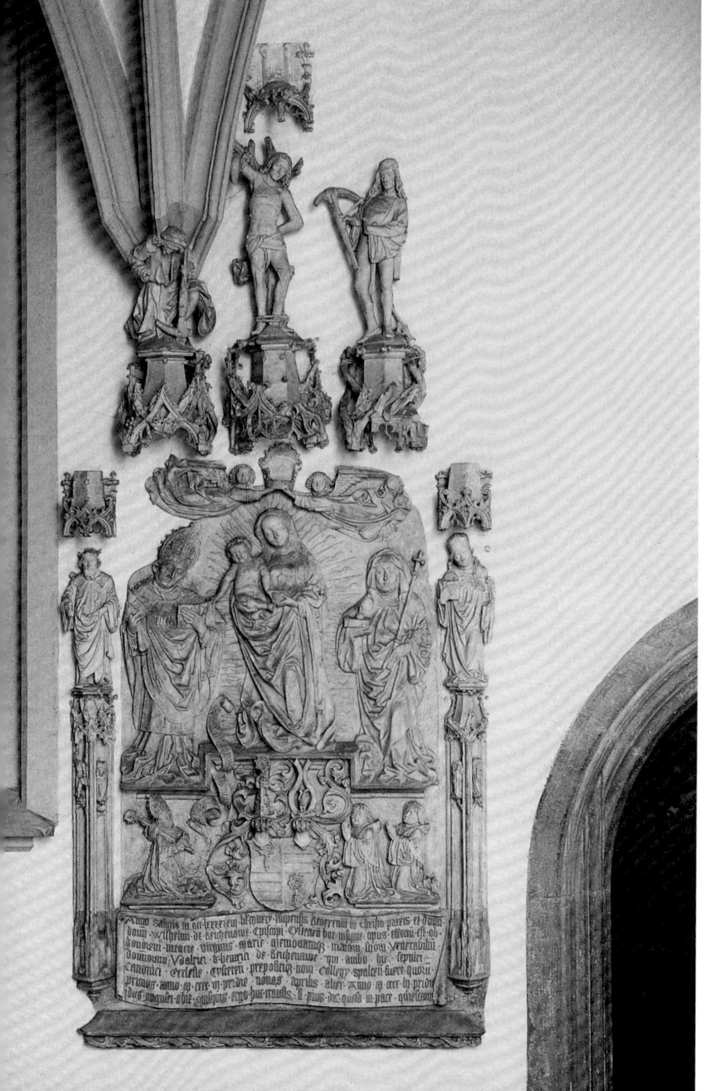

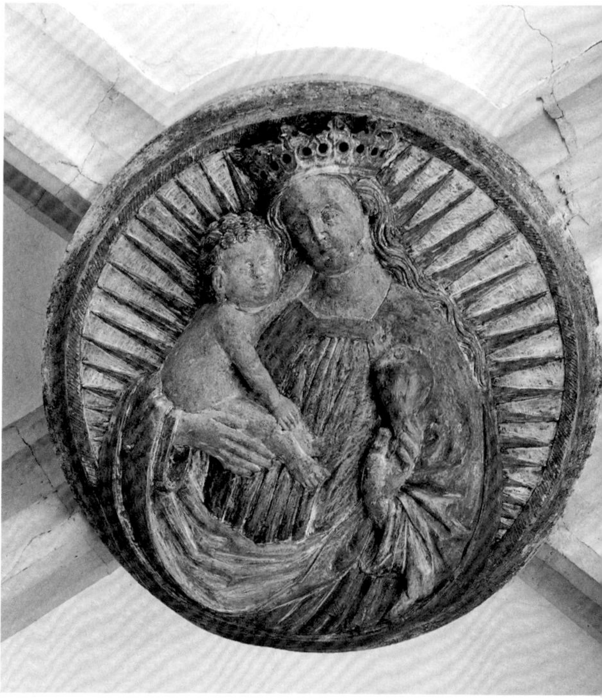

Figure 66. Epitaph of Wilhelm von Reichenau and his family, 1491. Limestone, 165 x 71 in. (42 x 18 cm). Mortuarium, Eichstätt Cathedral

Figure 67. *Virgin of the Apocalypse*, c. 1489. Carved and polychromed keystone. Mortuarium, Eichstätt Cathedral

Wilhelm ordered two carvings of the Virgin of the Apocalypse in the Mortuarium. In 1491 he commissioned his own impressive epitaph to honor Mary, as the accompanying inscription states (fig. 66).[89] Stylized portrayals of Wilhelm and two ancestors, Ulrich and Heinrich (d. 1446) von Reichenau, both former canons, kneel in adoration before the Virgin and Child. Wilhelm's prayer, written on the speech banderole, reads, "Ora pro nobis sanctus dei genitrix" (Pray for us Holy Mother of God).[90] Did the Kimbell statuette influence the design of the epitaph? Although it is difficult to prove a direct association, features such as the form of the crown, which is damaged in the epitaph, the positioning of Christ's legs with the left bent under the right, and the pose of Saint Walburga, who rather than Mary holds a scepter, are common to both works. Mary loosely recalls the Kimbell Virgin. Such similarities reflect the popularity of certain compositional types. Israhel van Meckenem's engraved *Virgin of the Apocalypse* shares many of the same traits, including the crowning angels (see fig. 16). In the epitaph, Mary is flanked by Saints Willibald and Walburga. Christ reaches down affectionately to touch Willibald's shoulder. Small statues of Saints Richard and Wunibald, along with four tiny figures, rendered unidentifiable because of damage, are situated under the adjoining baldachins. Saint Sebastian, tied to a tree, and two tormentors with their bows appear at the apex of the monument.[91] I suspect that an architectural frame originally united the various parts of this ensemble.

The Mortuarium's vault is decorated with sixteen carved and painted keystones, perhaps by the sculptor of the bishop's epitaph (fig. 67).[92] Appropriate to the hall's funerary function, the cycle shows the Last Judgment. Christ as judge is accompanied by trumpeting angels, saints (including the now-familiar Eichstätt quartet), and Death as a skeleton. Wilhelm is perpetually present. His coat of arms adorns the keystone of the first bay, where once a door permitted the canons direct access to the choir. The Virgin Mary and Saint Willibald, as his and the cathedral's patrons, appear on the adjoining keystones. These three bays are supported by the Beautiful Column, with Wilhelm's inscribed dedication.

Wilhelm is buried in the Willibald's choir immediately adjacent to the saint's own shrine (see figs. 56, 68). His funeral services included an early Mass and Prime in the Willibald's choir followed later by a Mass of Our Lady before the east choir.[93] He assumed his interment in the Willibald's choir would be brief, since he wished to be buried in a new adjoining Mary chapel, which was planned but never erected. Following custom, Wilhelm expected his successor to erect his tomb, just as he had done for Johann von Eich. Sometime before 1500, Bishop von Eyb, a sophisticated patron of the arts, commissioned Hans Beierlein (Peuerlin) of Augsburg, one of the region's foremost sculptors.[94] The expensive red-marble tomb depicts a Crucifixion set within a church with tall lancet windows. A bit incongruously, Christ's loincloth flutters in the breeze. Below, Bishop Wilhelm kneels staring at Christ. He prays, "Per tuas passionem miserere mei devs" (Through your passion, have mercy on me God). The bishop is introduced by his namesake, William the Hermit. The Virgin Mary, hands clasped tightly together,

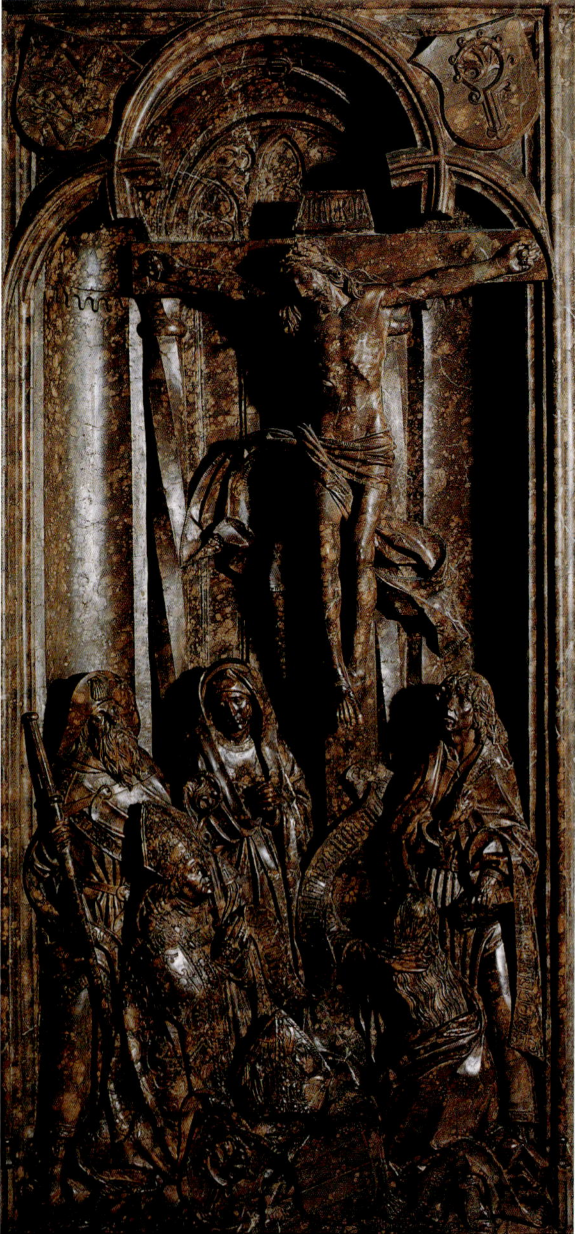

Figure 68. Hans Beierlein, Tomb of Wilhelm von Reichenau, before 1500. Marble, 106 x 53 in. (269.2 x 134.6 cm). Willibald's choir, Eichstätt Cathedral

stares not at her son but instead at Wilhelm, her devoted admirer. Opposite, Mary Magdalene, her hair unbound, poignantly clutches the cross while John the Evangelist grieves more silently.

Although a Marian chapel was never built, Wilhelm presumably took comfort knowing that a fourth example of the Virgin of the Apocalypse was nearby. In 1471 he reconsecrated the high altar to the Virgin Mary. Either he and/or the cathedral chapter erected the monumental high altar in the main, or eastern, choir (fig. 69).[95] Over-life-size polychromed wooden statues of the Virgin, holding her son and a scepter, and Saints Willibald (wearing the newly designed rational), Walburga, Richard, and Wunibald fill the center shrine. The original retable was dismantled in 1749 to make way for Matthias Seybold's new Rococo-style marble altar, with its own dramatic Virgin of the Apocalypse accompanied by Willibald and his family. This, in turn, was removed in 1883 and replaced the following year by the current neo-Gothic winged altar incorporating the original statues.

Figure 69. *Altar of the Virgin* (High Altar), 1470s–early 1480s. Limewood with modern polychromy, over-life-size shrine statues. Eichstätt Cathedral

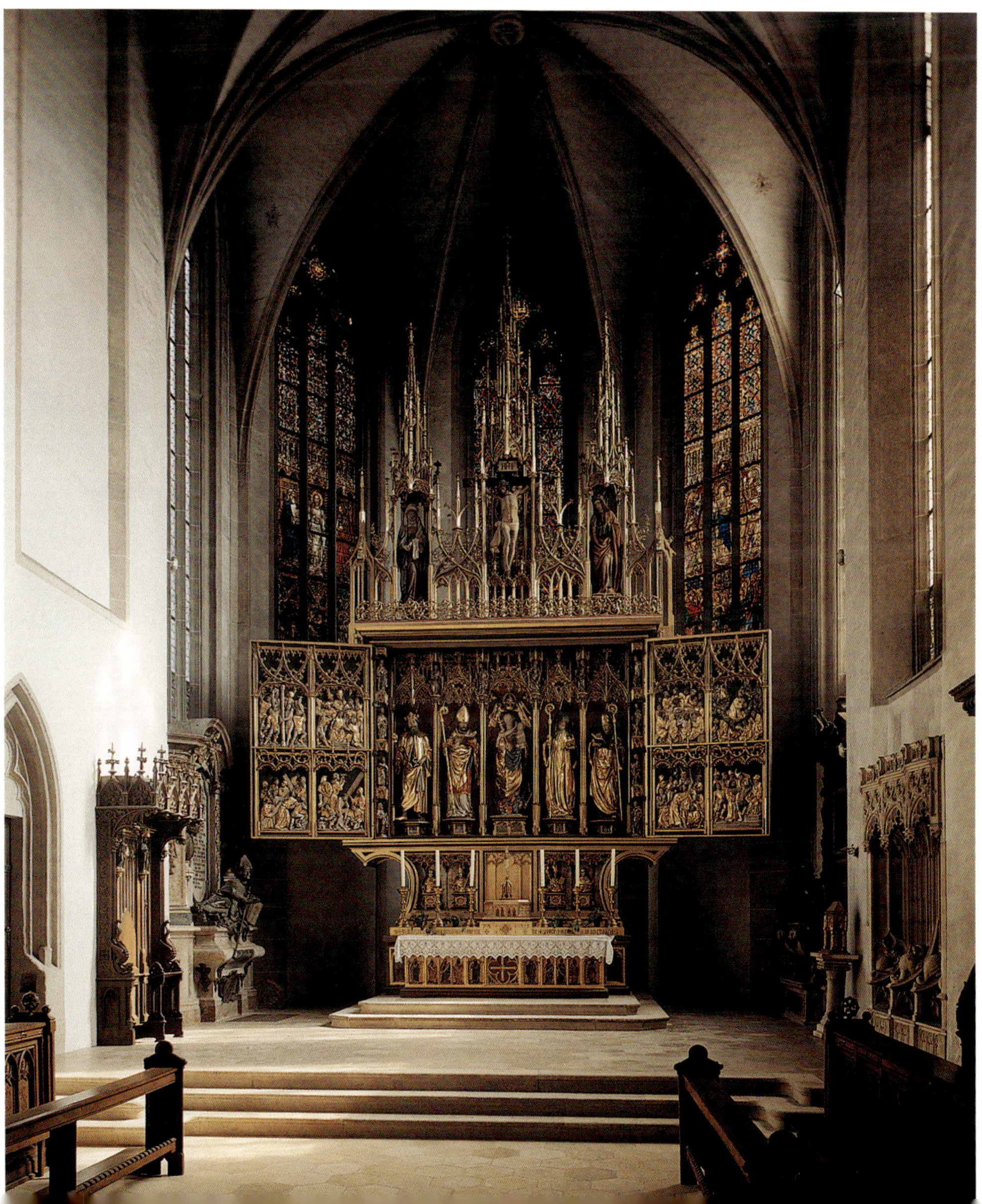

During his lifetime Wilhelm von Reichenau used the *Kimbell Virgin and Child* as a private devotional aid. Mary was the focus of many Catholic rituals including the recitation of the "Hail Mary," then one of the two foundational Christian prayers along with "Our Father." The text reads, "Hail Mary, full of grace, the Lord is with thee: blessed art thou amongst women, and blessed is the fruit of thy womb, Jesus. Holy Mary, Mother of God, pray for us sinners, now and at the hour of our death. Amen." This stresses Mary's uniqueness as God's chosen handmaiden, the physical vessel for realizing the incarnation, her role as mother of Jesus, and her power to intercede on behalf of the worshipper now and at the moment of one's death. Briefly, let us consider each of these aspects.

As recounted in the Gospel according to Luke (1:26–38), God picked Mary to bear his son. When Archangel Gabriel announced this news to the young woman, the Word became flesh even though she remained a virgin. Mary was truly "alone of all her sex," to borrow Marina Warner's felicitous book title, because she alone was both a virgin and a mother.[96] This singularity fascinated, indeed obsessed, clergy and laity alike. While most of this subject is beyond the scope of the present discussion, one aspect is relevant. During the Middle Ages, theologians argued not over Mary's sinlessness but over when she became sinless.[97] The Maculists, especially the Dominicans, claimed that Mary, like all humans, was tainted by Original Sin, mankind's fall through Adam and Eve; however, she was purified of all sin while in the womb of Saint Anne, her mother. The Immaculists, led by the Franciscans, countered that Mary, through God's grace, had been sinless (or immaculate) since the instant of her own conception. This long-simmering and remarkably vitriolic dispute exploded during the middle of Bishop Wilhelm's reign. In 1477, Pope Sixtus IV (r. 1471–84), a Franciscan, ordered a formal debate between the two sides in Rome. Favoring the Immaculists' position, the pontiff soon afterward established the Office for the Feast of the Conception of the Immaculate Virgin on December 8; in 1480 he added the Feast of the Immaculate Conception. As the opponents continued to disagree, Sixtus issued a papal bull, *Grave Nimis*, in 1485, stating that since the Roman Church and Apostolic See had not ruled on the doctrine of the Immaculate Conception, neither position could be called heretical. Wielding the threat of excommunication, the pontiff sought to calm both sides. The Catholic Church approved the doctrine of the Immaculate Conception only in 1854.

In 1476 and 1477, Sixtus IV further encouraged belief in the Immaculate Conception by offering an indulgence of eleven thousand years for recitation of the prayer: "Ave, Sanctissima Maria mater dei regina celi porta paradisi, . . ." (Hail Most Holy Mary, Mother of God, Queen of Heaven, Gate of Paradise, . . .).[98] Although other Marian subjects were occasionally linked with the Immaculate Conception, it was the Virgin of the Apocalypse or, frequently in half-length, *Maria in Sole* that became the definitive image associated with this doctrine. In another engraving Israhel van Meckenem printed this prayer and indulgence along with his Marian image (fig. 70).[99]

Mary embodied the human side of Christianity. Fifteenth-century art stressed not just every episode of her life but, on a more universal level, how her experiences as Jesus's mother deepened her understanding of and empathy for others. She bore a child only to see him crucified. This point is explicit in van Meckenem's other engraving, showing Mary carrying her son in her left arm and holding a crucifix with Christ's nailed body in her right hand (see fig. 16). Christ is both fleshy child and bloody sacrifice. Her seven joys and seven sorrows were the subjects of one's meditations, especially as the often overlapping cult of the rosary was being fervently practiced at this time.[100]

The *Kimbell Virgin and Child* is an iconic image, one outside the limits of conventional time and strict biblical narrative. Mary is now Queen of Heaven and the personification of Ecclesia or the Church. For Bishop Wilhelm and his contemporaries, Mary was indeed the Gate of Paradise. Van Meckenem

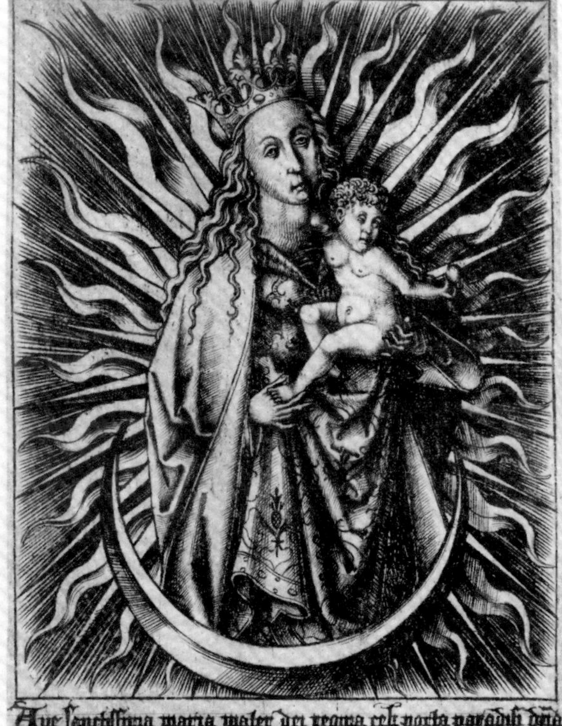

Figure 70. Israhel van Meckenem, *Virgin of the Apocalypse*, c. 1490s (?). Engraving, 5⅝ x 4⁷⁄₁₆ in. (14.2 x 11.2 cm). Staatliche Kunstsammlungen, Dresden (A 1926-303)

inscribed the banderole over Mary's head with the words, "Who correctly comprehends me will have eternal life" (Sirach 24:31). The worshipper prayed to Mary, hoping for her merciful intercession on earth and in heaven. Consider two stained-glass windows in the Mortuarium. In the *Last Judgment*, Mary, kneeling at Christ's right, advocates for the individual's salvation (fig. 71).[101] In his epitaph located beside this window, Wilhelm pleads, "Pray for us Holy Mother of God." Nearby Mary is represented as the *Schutzmantel Madonna* (fig. 72).[102] She stands with her cloak outstretched, protecting the devout huddled beneath from divine wrath over human sinfulness. Being sinless, Mary also triumphs over the devil, as personified by the serpent-tailed Eve holding an apple in van Meckenem's engraving (see fig. 16). The final two inscriptions in this print champion Mary's immaculate conception.

Bishop Wilhelm's devotion to the Virgin did not require an image. Although the goal for many Christians was imageless prayer and meditation, a work of art was commonly employed as a catalyst.

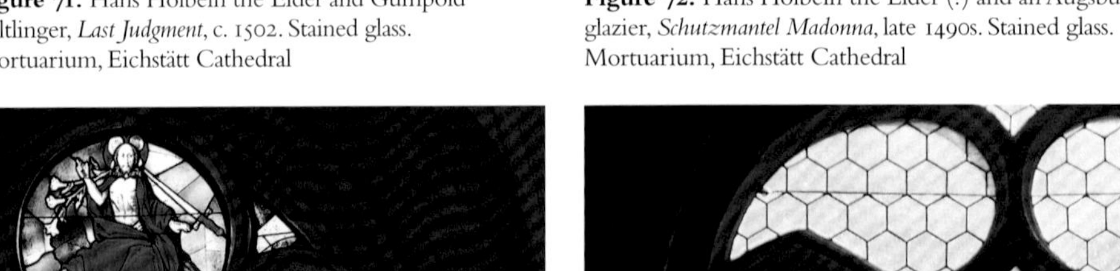

Figure 71. Hans Holbein the Elder and Gumpold Giltlinger, *Last Judgment*, c. 1502. Stained glass. Mortuarium, Eichstätt Cathedral

Figure 72. Hans Holbein the Elder (?) and an Augsburg glazier, *Schutzmantel Madonna*, late 1490s. Stained glass. Mortuarium, Eichstätt Cathedral

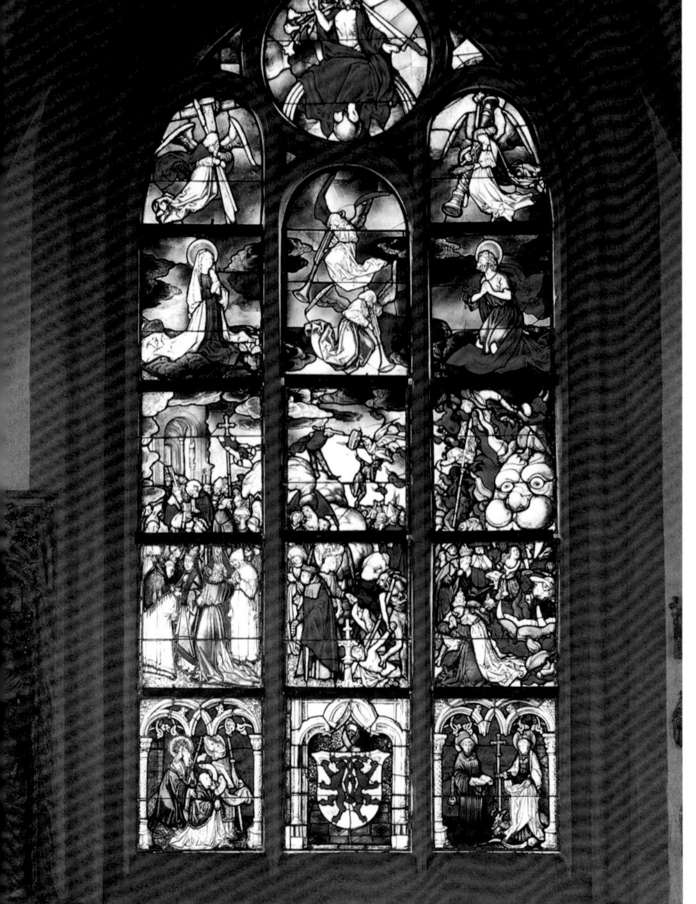

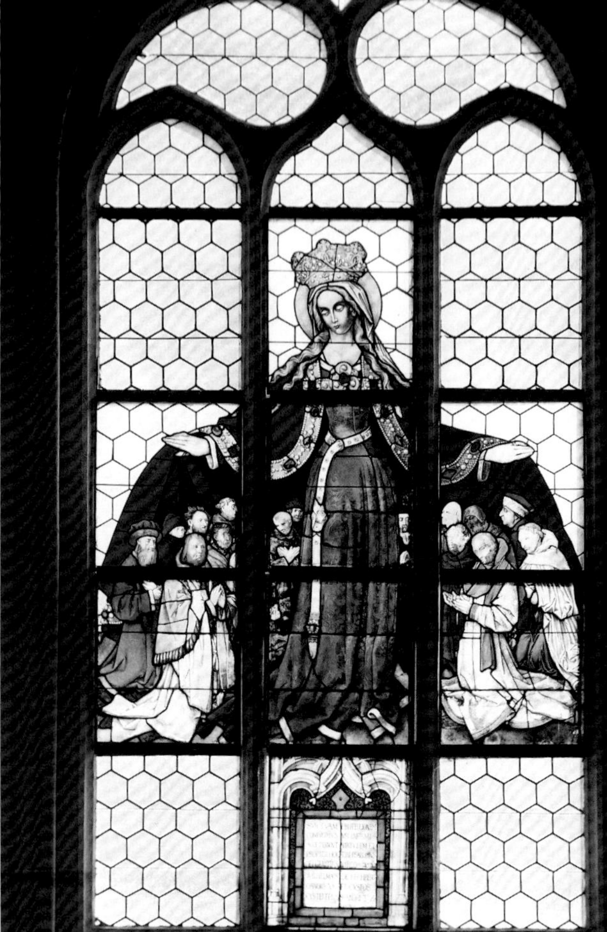

Sight, the strongest of all the senses, stimulates memory and promotes spiritual insight.[103] Examination leads to contemplation; that is, by looking at the statuette, Wilhelm could recall Mary's life and her many different roles. It puts human faces, albeit artistically conceived ones, on the Virgin and her infant son.

The statuette placed on an altar provided a locus for his daily devotional routine, such as the recitation of litanies extolling Mary or the celebration of the Little Office of the Blessed Virgin Mary (or the Hours of the Virgin). As explained succinctly by Roger Wieck, "There are eight separate Hours: Matins, Lauds, Prime, Terce, Sext, None, Vespers, and Compline. Each Hour consists mostly of Psalms, plus varying combinations of hymns, prayers, and readings (lessons), to which innumerable short ejaculations (antiphons, versicles, and responses) are generously sprinkled. . . . Repeated on a daily basis from childhood to old age, the Hours of the Virgin became a familiar, steadfast friend."[104] The accompanying responses honor Mary:

> O holy and immaculate Virgin, with what praises I shall extol thee, I know not:
> for he whom the heavens could not contain rested in thy bosom.

> Blessed art thou, O Virgin Mary, who didst bear the Lord, the Creator of the
> world: thou hast brought forth him who made thee, and thou remainest a
> virgin for ever.

> Truly thou art happy, O holy Virgin Mary, and most worthy of all praise:
> for out of thee is risen the sun of justice, Christ our God.[105]

Wilhelm, desiring eternal life, was familiar with the prevailing economy of salvation, specifically the belief that earthly actions could positively, or negatively, affect Christ's final judgment of one's soul. Besides petitioning Mary and the saints for their positive intercession, one sought to lessen the length of time spent in purgatory.[106] Catholics believe that most people, excluding the damned, enter purgatory upon dying. They remain in this place of fire until their sins are atoned for. During the half century prior to the advent of the Protestant Reformation (1517), the Catholic Church granted an ever-increasing number of indulgences, temporal credits that lessened the length of one's stay in purgatory. Wilhelm occasionally authorized indulgences, such as those granted in 1488 and 1490 to anyone visiting or supporting the new Marienburg convent.[107] According to the *Wittenberger Heiltumsbuch* (1509), a visitor to the Schlosskirche in Wittenberg could earn a total of 1,443 years of indulgence when Elector Friedrich the Wise's 5,005-piece relic collection was on display (see fig. 54).[108]

Some individuals kept scrupulous track of their growing account of grace. For example, Albrecht von Brandenburg, archbishop of Mainz (r. 1514–45), reckoned that his collection of relics in the collegiate church in Halle merited an indulgence equaling 39,245,120 years of penance.[109]

Bishop Wilhelm's exact motivations for commissioning the *Kimbell Virgin and Child* can only be surmised. Yet when this exquisite silver statuette is situated within the context of his other commissions for Eichstätt Cathedral, a clear picture emerges of his profound devotion to the Virgin Mary, Christ, and the four locally venerated saints. If his interest in architecture is any indication, Wilhelm appreciated, and paid dearly for, the aesthetic beauty of this statuette. He treasured and used it daily as a spiritual aid.

The *Kimbell Virgin and Child* as a Collector's Object

According to the *Pontifikale Gundekarianum*, cited above, Bishop Wilhelm gave his statuette to the cathedral, presumably upon his death in 1496. The cathedral chapter stored its treasures in the sacristy (fig. 73). Occasionally, it would have been set on an altar for liturgical services. The next secure refer-

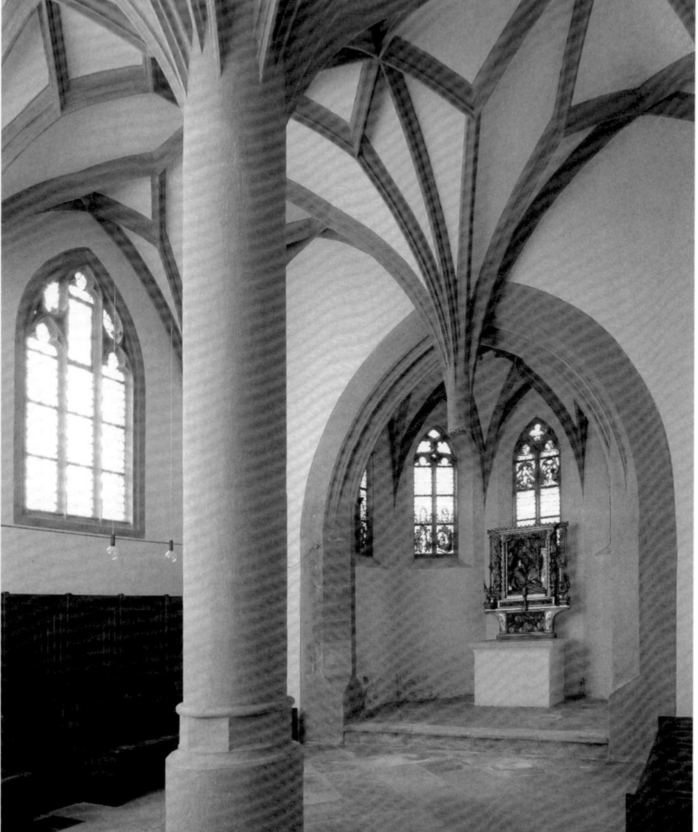

Figure 73. Sacristy, 1463/64–80. Eichstätt Cathedral

ence to the *Kimbell Virgin and Child* occurs in Ferdinand Luthmer's 1885 catalogue of the collection of Mayer Carl von Rothschild in Frankfurt (fig. 74). Its intervening history is unknown, though one can make certain assumptions. During the Protestant Reformation, Eichstätt remained Catholic, so neither the city nor its cathedral experienced the sort of iconoclasm that destroyed so much German art during the 1520s and 1530s. Eichstätt, however, was not spared during the Thirty Years' War

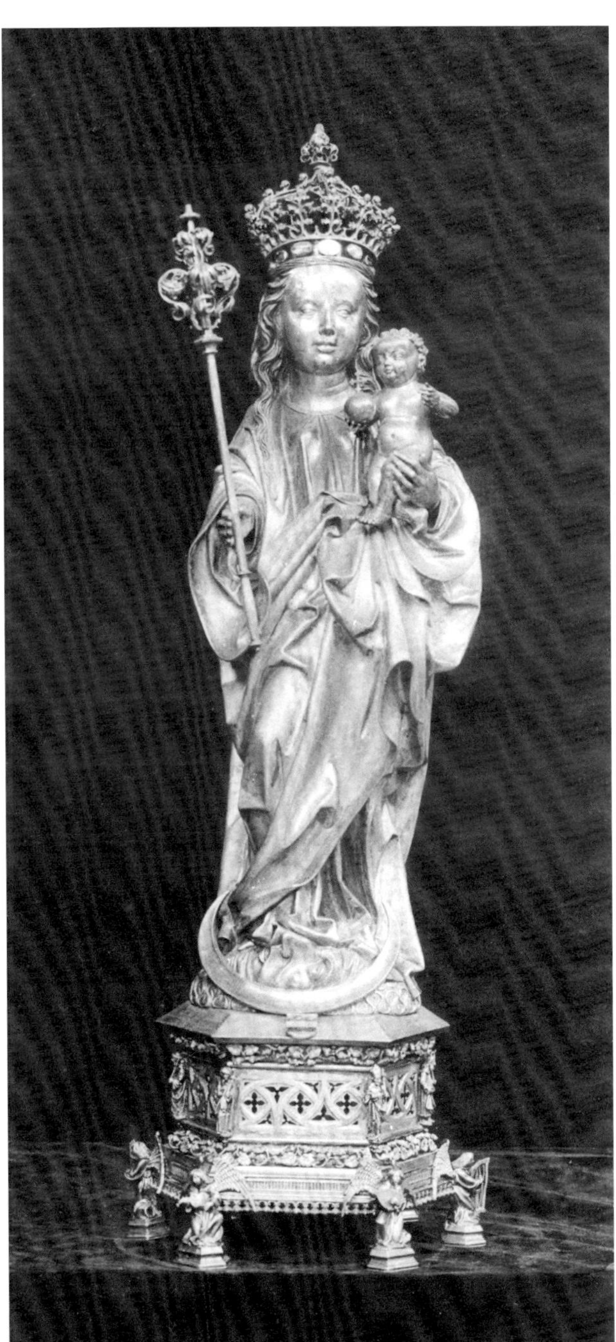

Figure 74. *The Kimbell Virgin and Child*, 1885. Photograph in Mayer Carl von Rothschild's collection in Frankfurt, from Luthmer 1883–85, vol. 2, plate XVI, printed in reverse. Germanisches Nationalmuseum, Nuremberg (2° K 2393g)

(1618–48), when in 1633 and 1634 the city was occupied by Swedish and German Protestant troops.[110] On December 7, 1633, the soldiers destroyed 444, or 77 percent, of Eichstätt's houses and six churches, including that of the Jesuits, then under construction. The cathedral was saved, but the adjoining bishop's palace, which Wilhelm had built, the nearby provost's house, and its chapel of Saint Veit were razed. Carrying its treasures, presumably including the *Kimbell Virgin and Child*, the canons fled to nearby Ingolstadt, with its massive fortifications. Many valuable objects were given to the Swedish troops to pay the occupation tax. The Kimbell statuette was very probably back in Eichstätt by or before 1648, when the Treaty of Westphalia, signed in Münster, ended the war. Did the Kimbell statuette inspire Johann Jakob Berg's copper *Virgin of the Apocalypse* (1778–80), which triumphantly stands on the tall stone column of the Mary Fountain in the square before the bishop's palace in Eichstätt?[111] The two works share many of the same design features.

The Kimbell Virgin and Child was threatened again in 1799–1806.[112] French troops led by Field Marshall Michel Ney occupied Eichstätt on July 14, 1800. Dominik Joba, another French general, stole the bishop's painting collection, which filled five wagons, and much of the libraries of the cathedral and Kloster Rebdorf. Eichstätt was controlled by the French until 1803, the Austrians until December 26, 1805, and then the king of Bavaria. Each change in rule further impoverished the town, the diocese, and their artistic patrimony. In late 1802 the process of secularization began; church property was seized and then sold by the state.[113] On October 27, 1805, Archduke Ferdinand of Austria demanded that gold, silver, and other precious objects should be "placed on the altar of the Fatherland"; that is, sent to him. Bishop Joseph I of Eichstätt pawned some items and ordered the melting of chalices and other church metalworks to pay this new war tax.[114] The Bavarian government moved quickly in 1806 to secure and then liquidate church property throughout the diocese.

During these tumultuous years, many works of religious art, likely including the *Kimbell Virgin and Child*, were displaced and sold. The Cistercian monastery at Kaisheim lost its goldsmith treasures in 1803–6 (see figs. 36, 38, 52). The *Virgin and Child* from Saint Moritz in Augsburg is documented leaving the parish church in 1806 only to be given back, minus its base and reverse, by a local clergyman in 1821 (see fig. 51).[115] When Eichstätt's church of Unserer Lieben Frau was dissolved in 1808, a local church administrator acquired Seld's silver altar (see fig. 53).[116] King Ludwig I of Bavaria purchased the altar from another local cleric in 1835. Interestingly, once these objects left their churches, their status often changed from a functioning example of devotional or liturgical art to a work of art. That is, these items became collectible objects admired primarily for their aesthetic merits. The early nineteenth century, not surprisingly, marked the emergence of new private collections and public museums across Germany.[117]

Precisely how and when the *Kimbell Virgin and Child* left Eichstätt may never be known. Similarly, it is unclear when and where Mayer Carl von Rothschild (1820–1886) of Frankfurt acquired the statuette. Mayer Carl, often called Charles, was an important, third-generation member of the Rothschild investment family (fig. 75).[118] In the sixteenth century his ancestors moved to Frankfurt, where, as Jews, they were restricted to a single ghetto, known as the Judengasse. The family once lived in a house called Zum roten Schild (beside the red shield), from which their descendents eventually derived the name Rothschild. The firm was established by Mayer Carl's grandfather, Amschel Mayer (1744–1812), and his five sons, each of whom was responsible for business in a different part of Europe. Mayer Carl, a grandson, ran the Frankfurt branch. He was named Prussian court banker in 1860 and was elected to the parliament of the North German Federation in 1867.

In 1846, four years after marrying Louise de Rothschild (1820–1894), his British first cousin, Mayer Carl purchased the impressive classical-style house at Untermainkai 15, a desirable location facing the Main River (fig. 76).[119] It was constructed in 1820–21 for Joseph Isaak Speyer, one of the first wealthy Jews permitted to live outside the Judengasse. Over the next four or five years, architect Fried-

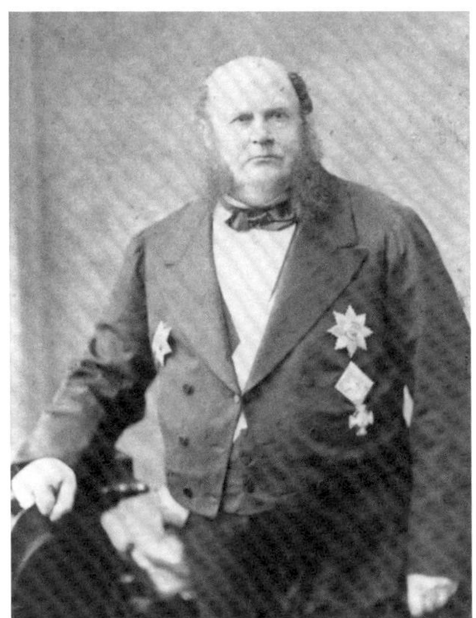

Figure 75. *Mayer Carl von Rothschild.* Photograph, c. 1870

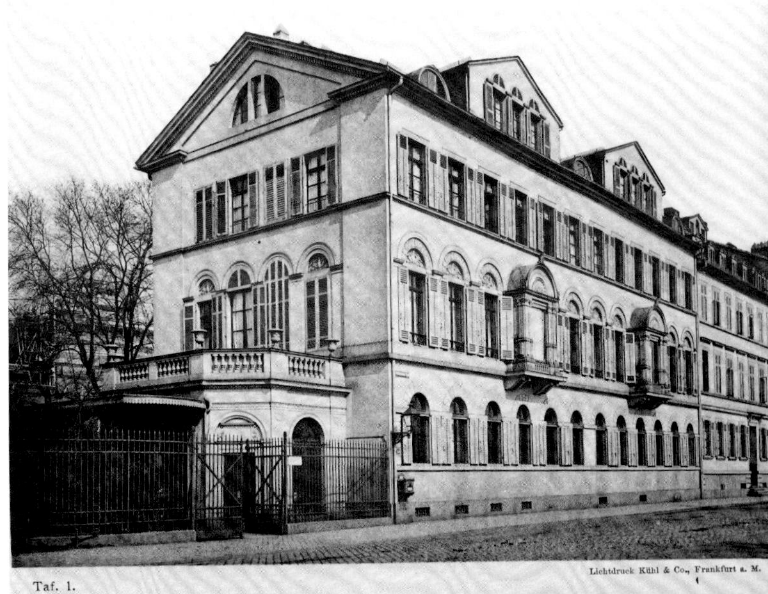

Figure 76. House of Mayer Carl von Rothschild, Untermainkai 15, Frankfurt am Main. Photograph, c. 1891–1900. Historisches Museum, Frankfurt am Main

rich Rumpf expanded the house by an additional five bays and erected three showy rooms on the ground floor: the smoking room, done in Louis XIV-style with wood paneling, fluted columns, and a coffered ceiling; the music room, outfitted in a gold-and-white Louis XV-style; and a smaller salon in a classicizing Louis XVI-style. He also possessed Schloss Bornburg at Bornheim, outside Frankfurt, a gift from his father, Carl Mayer, in about 1840. Almost immediately Mayer Carl commissioned Rumpf to construct Günthersburg, a new Italian Renaissance-style country villa, in its place.[120]

During these years Mayer Carl started buying art. At a time when French art dominated European taste, he favored older German art, especially goldsmith objects. His most impressive acquisition, made only in 1880, was Wenzel Jamnitzer's silver *Merkel Table Decoration*, arguably the finest extant northern-European goldsmith work of the sixteenth century (fig. 77).[121] Long owned by Nuremberg's city council as an example of the brilliance of its artists, this dish was intended to be admired, not used. The personification of Mother Earth stands surrounded by minute grasses and small creatures cast from life. She supports a basin ornamented with more animals, plants, putti, strapwork, and other decorative forms. This was a conversation piece, a virtuoso juxtaposition of natural and man-made artifice. Mayer Carl displayed his goldsmith works and other treasures, arranged generally by materials, in freestanding glass cabinets in his town house as well as at Günthersburg. When Ferdinand Luthmer, a Frankfurt art historian, catalogued the collection in 1885, Mayer Carl owned over three thousand items ranging from coins and watches to paintings and expensive furnishings.[122]

Mayer Carl purchased his art from various art dealers and antiquarians. One probable source was the Pickert family.[123] Abraham Pickert, assisted by his sons, was a leading supplier of late medieval and Renaissance German art. Based initially in Fürth, he moved to Albrecht Dürer Platz 10 in Nuremberg in 1854. The firm's visitor books for 1838–1909, excluding 1881–94, are in the Stadtarchiv in Nuremberg. The guests included nobility, museum directors and curators, scholars and artists, and some of the most notable European and American collectors of the era. On July 29, 1842, the twenty-two-year-old Mayer Carl, his father, and two of his London cousins visited Pickert in Fürth. Nothing else is known about this occasion, though it indicates that the Rothschilds were in the market for art. One wonders how this trip to the Pickerts and, doubtlessly, other antiquarians affected Mayer Carl, who a few years later bought art for his two houses. Mayer Carl stopped by the Nuremberg establishment in September 1877. The Pickerts scoured German sources for paintings, manuscripts, stained-glass windows, sculptures, goldsmith works, and a host of other objects for their clients. Another visitor, Jakob Falke of Vienna, curator at the Germanisches Nationalmuseum in Nuremberg (1855–58), remarked in his autobiography that Pickert was among the most important dealers who took advantage of the beautiful and old works of art that appeared on the market after the breaking up of the Bavarian monasteries. Pickert also kept some of the finest objects for himself.

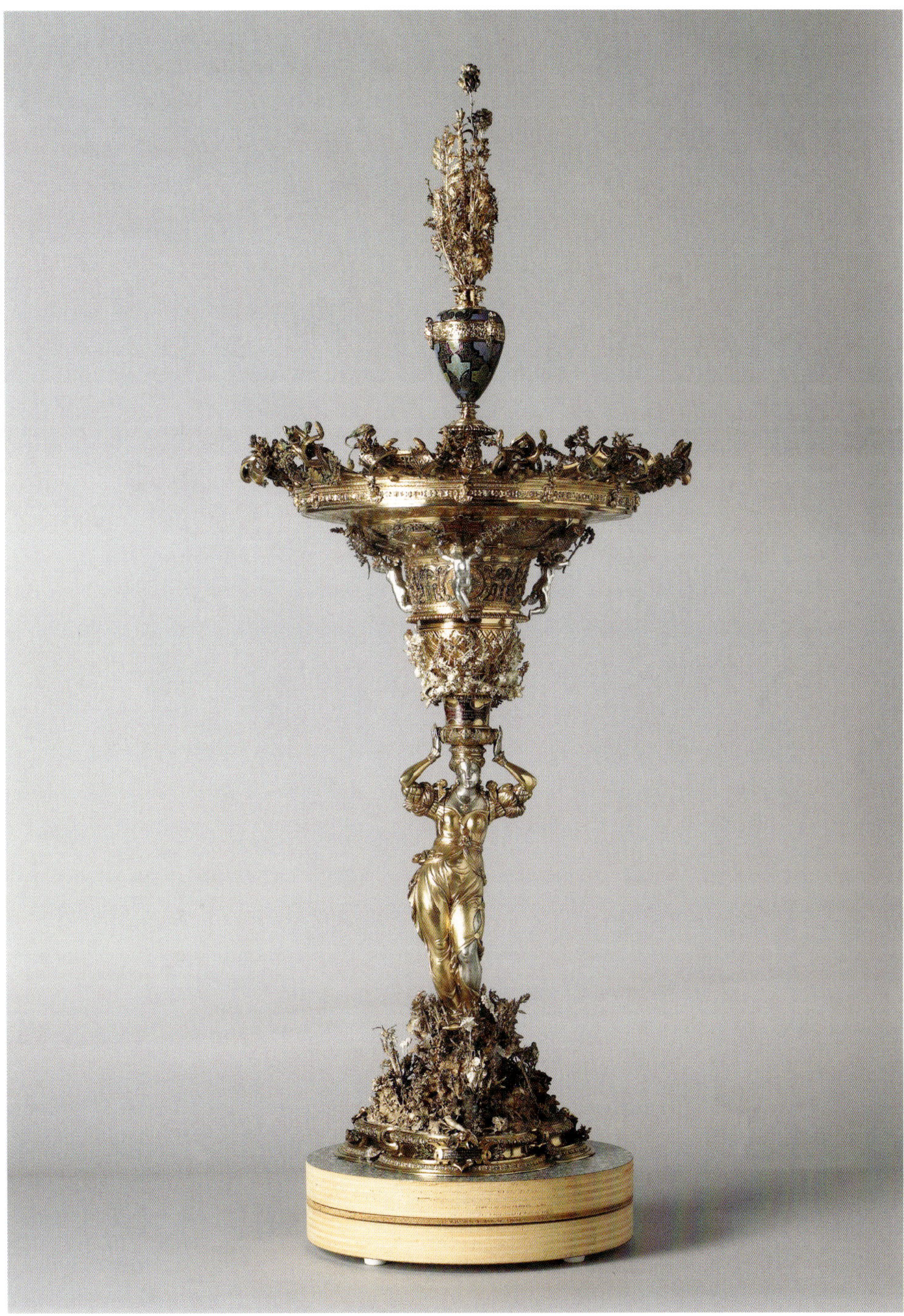

Figure 77. Wenzel Jamnitzer, *Merkel Table Decoration*, 1549. Silver with gilt and polychromed enamel, 39¼ x 18⅛ in. (99.8 x 46 cm). Rijksmuseum, Amsterdam

Upon Mayer Carl's death in 1886, his widow, Louise, instructed Selig Goldschmidt, Luthmer, and their assistants to inventory the collection and divide the contents into five equal parts. The *Kimbell Virgin and Child*, then displayed at Günthersburg, is listed as number 65a: "Madonna with Child, on a crescent moon, . . . on a pierced Gothic socle, which is carried by little musical angel figures, the crown is set with noble stones. Height 54 cm."[124] The statuette was included in the fifth grouping, which became the property of Hannah Louise (1850–92), the couple's unmarried daughter, who lived in Frankfurt with her mother. Hannah Louise was well known for supporting charitable causes. In 1890 she opened the family house to the public for three hours weekly in the winter and six hours weekly in the summer. In 1895, a year after the mother's death, the house became a public library and since 1988 has been Frankfurt's Jewish Museum.[125]

The *Kimbell Virgin and Child* passed to Hannah's sister, Laura Thérèse (1847–1931), who lived in Paris.[126] Next, Henri James Nathaniel Charles (1872–1947), her only surviving child, probably inherited it. The statuette remained in the family's possession until the late 1960s. It was purchased by Daniel Katz Ltd., of London, in 2002 and finally sold to the Kimbell Art Foundation.

Mayer Carl von Rothschild was one of the leading private collectors in nineteenth-century Germany. He possessed the *Kimbell Virgin and Child* and Jamnitzer's *Merkel Table Decoration*, two of the greatest German goldsmith works. His holdings compared favorably with those of famed princely collections in Dresden, Munich, and Vienna. Items from his collection today grace many major museums, including the Rijksmuseum in Amsterdam, Landesmusem in Karlsruhe, Bayerisches Nationalmuseum in Munich, Metropolitan Museum of Art in New York, Germanisches Nationalmuseum in Nuremberg, Ashmolean Museum in Oxford, and Musée de Cluny in Paris.[127]

The *Kimbell Virgin and Child* has had a remarkable history. It was created originally as an expression of Wilhelm von Reichenau's devotion to the Virgin Mary. The bishop bequeathed his treasured goldsmith work to Eichstätt Cathedral and its chapter of canons. The political upheavals around 1800 cast the statuette into the marketplace, where its physical beauty rather than its spiritual efficaciousness now was paramount. Subsequently, it was acquired by Mayer Carl von Rothschild, a member of Europe's foremost banking family, who delighted in displaying his art collection to guests.[128] After a couple of centuries of wandering, the *Virgin and Child* now has found a permanent home in Fort Worth, where this once deeply private object may be admired by all who visit the Kimbell Art Museum.

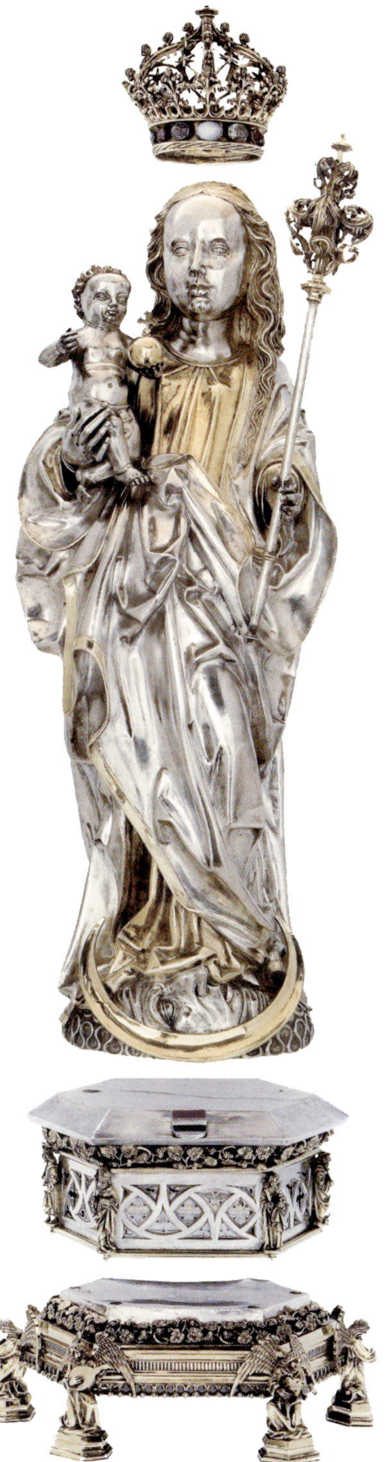

Figure 78. *The Kimbell Virgin and Child*, disassembled parts

For their assistance, I wish to thank Timothy Potts, Nancy E. Edwards, Claire M. Barry, Malcolm Warner, Wendy P. Gottlieb, Lindsay E. Askins, Tom Dawson, and Robert LaPrelle of the Kimbell Art Museum; the Fortson Family and the Kimbell Art Foundation (Fort Worth); John W. O'Malley (Boston); John Dennis (Dallas); Lawrence Nichols (Toledo); Glenn Peers (Austin); Larry Silver (Philadelphia); Christina Corsiglia and Kenneth Thomson (Toronto); Melanie Thierbach (Augsburg); Emanuel Braun (Eichstätt); Norbert Jopek (London); Willibald Sauerländer (Munich); and Stefan Roller (Ulm).

NOTES

1. *Pontifikale Gundekarianum* (Eichstätt MS B4), fol. 42; Suttner 1867, pp. 19–20, here 19.

2. The announcement appeared on the Museum's Web site (www.kimbellart.org) as well as in the *New York Times* (Carol Vogel, "Rarities for Fort Worth," Inside Art, *New York Times*, Weekend section: Fine Arts, Leisure, September 6, 2002) and the *Dallas Morning News* (Janet Kutner, "Kimbell Buys Gothic Rarity," *Dallas Morning News*, Metropolitan section: Overnight, September 6, 2002), among other newspapers. The statuette adorned the cover of *The Burlington Magazine* 144, no. 1197 (December 2002) and p. 789. Potts 2003, pp. 38–39 [Nancy E. Edwards].

3. Luthmer 1883–85, vol. 2, pl. XVI. Also Luthmer 1890, p. 82; Lüdke 1983, vol. 1, p. 77, and vol. 2, pp. 434–35, no. 102; Ulm 2002, no. 42 [Norbert Jopek].

4. Hollstein (1954–), vols. 24–24a, no. 200; Geissmar and Louis 1995, p. 329.

5. Van Os et al. 2000, pp. 123–31, figs. 150–61.

6. Braunfels 1979–89, vol. 2, pp. 217–28. Biller 2001, pp. 25–35; Marsch, Biller, and Jacob 2001, vol. 1, pl. R49/A3; vol. 2, pp. 37–42, 405–15.

7. The order of the figures starting at the front right and moving clockwise is Saints Walburga, Willibald, Richard, John the Evangelist, William the Hermit, and Wunibald. Appel, Braun, and Hofmann 1987, pp. 31–37, 103–13, 125–26.

8. Kirschbaum and Braunfels 1968–76, vol. 8, cols. 607–12. A similarly dressed Saint William appears with Canon Wilhelm von Rechberg in a 1502 window designed by Hans Holbein the Elder in the Mortuarium of Eichstätt Cathedral. Mader 1924, p. 188, pl. XVII; Frenzel 1968, p. 11. Frenzel misidentifies Saint William as Saint Richard; however, he plausibly suggests that these glass panels originally belonged with the nearby *Last Judgment* window.

9. Füssel 2005. The size of a single page is 16½ x 12⅝ in. (42 x 32 cm.). On Northern European art of this period, see Smith 2004.

10. Wilson 1976; Smith 1983, pp. 94–95. One could purchase the book printed on parchment or paper, bound or unbound, and with or without hand-colored woodcuts. Eichstätt is on fol. 162 recto in both editions.

11. Wilson 1976, pp. 208–9, 217. The copy is in Schedel's own Latin edition of the chronicle (Munich, Bayerische Staatsbibliothek, Cim. 187, fol. 2, of the prefatory pages).

12. Schoch, Mende, and Scherbaum 2002, pp. 59–105, especially no. 121. As an historical aside, Dürer's best friend, Willibald Pirckheimer, was born in Eichstätt in 1470 and was named after the diocese's main patron saint. His father, Johann, served as Bishop Wilhelm's legal counsel and secretary from 1466 until 1475. Neuhofer 1971.

13. Hernad 1990; Landau and Parshall 1994.

14. On this painting and the period's international exchange of art, see Nuttall 2004, especially pp. 60–69, pls. 1, 63–65.

15. Aikema and Brown 2000, no. 48; Potts 2003, pp. 36–37. It has been suggested that the painting was made for Eleonora of Aragon.

16. Steinberg 1996.

17. Lightbown 1989, pp. 152–63.

18. Schwemmer 1973, pp. 222–49.

19. Fritz 1982, pp. 31–36.

20. Cherry 1992, pp. 18–21, figs. 14–15.

21. Bern 1979, no. 69; Fritz 1982, pp. 14, 43–44, pl. I.

22. Huth 1967 generally on guilds, contracts, work-shops, and other related issues for all the visual arts of this period. Cherry 1992, pp. 24–32; Thierbach 2003, pp. 29–38.

23. Tanner 1991, pp. 7–16.

24. Augsburg 1965, no. 172; and Tanner 1991, no. 63.

25. Hollstein 1954–, vols. 24–24a, nos. 587–587a; Tanner 1991, no. 72.

26. Augsburg 1965, no. 64. Rowlands with Bartrum 1993, no. 300 verso, pl. 197.

27. Augsburg 1965, no. 276. See Jopek 2002, p. 75; and Norbert Jopek in Ulm 2002, p. 156, figs. 137–38. Jopek informs me that at some later date the statuette was turned 180 degrees on its base.

28. The polychromy is twentieth century in date. Augsburg 1965, no. 248; Ulm 2002, no. 28.

29. Augsburg 1965, no. 267; Lüdke 1983, p. 122, no. K 13; Ulm 2002, no. 29. Hufnagel's inscription is the oldest example for any Augsburg goldsmith; see Rosenberg 1922–25, vol. 1, p. 24, no. 113.

30. The comments that follow are based upon my observations and especially on the detailed technical report that Peter Dandridge prepared for the Kimbell Art Museum on March 10, 2003. I had the opportunity to study the disassembled statuette on March 3, 2006, while it was being cleaned by John Dennis, objects conservator of the Dallas Museum of Art. I wish to thank Claire M. Barry, chief conservator of the Kimbell Art Museum, and John Dennis for sharing their technical expertise. The base bears an engraved inscription: 13 mark 7 lot = weight. A useful discussion of goldsmith techniques is Sauter 2001.

31. Seling 1980, vol. 1, pp. 35–36, around 1500.

32. Rosenberg 1922–25.

33. One mark equals about 225 grams, or 8 ounces. Rosenberg 1922–25, vol. 3, pp. 343–58, especially 343–45. On p. 343 he refers incorrectly to Hans Greiff of Ingolstadt as an Ulm goldsmith. See fig. 47 in the present volume.

34. Rosenberg 1922–25, vol. 1, pp. 23–242, especially 23–29.

35. Rosenberg 1922–25, vol. 3, pp. 11–31.

36. Meininghaus 2000, pp. 1076–78.

37. About one work in six is dated. Fritz 1982, pp. 96, 111–12.

38. Fritz 1982, pp. 325–39. Augsburg had about eighty goldsmiths registered between 1466 and 1527. Eichstätt had only two known in the first half of the fifteenth century and seven traceable during the next seventy-five years. Ingolstadt averaged five masters active at any time during this period. Cologne had eighty masters in 1480 and seventy in 1500. Munich possessed twenty-three masters in 1472. Strasbourg had seventy-five masters and Würzburg sixty masters from around 1450 to 1525.

39. Hofmann 1992, p. 115; Lüdke 1983, no. 81; van Os et al. 2000, pp. 126–28, figs. 157–58.

40. Müllner made six statuettes for Friedrich the Wise in 1501–3; Bruck 1903, pp. 219–20, 312; see fig. 54 in the present volume. In 1517–18, Tilman Riemenschneider of Würzburg carved a wooden model for a bust of Saint Kilian that Müllner modified and cast for Würzburg Cathedral. Kohlhaussen 1968, pp. 283–93; Lüdke 1983, p. 129; New York and Nuremberg 1986, no. 52, for discussion of attribution problems.

41. Jakob Kobold, Michael Beck, Georg Gekirch, Ulrich Kigeln, Vinzenz Glaser, and Georg Fränklin each enrolled five or more pupils during this period. I derived my figures from Häberle 1934, pp. 30–32.

42. Fritz 1982, pp. 38, 334.

43. Meininghaus 2000, p. 1077.

44. I searched for Wilhelm's personal and episcopal payment records, any last will or testament, and cathedral chapter accounts that might pertain to the statuette's gifting.

45. Luthmer 1883–85, vol. 2, pl. XVI.

46. Lüdke 1983, pp. 434–35, no. 102.

47. He offers the Libyan Sibyl on the choir stalls in Ulm's Münster as a general comparison. Jopek

in Ulm 2002, no. 42; and Gropp 1999, pp. 108–9, fig. 81.

48. Conversation in London on April 5, 2005.

49. For Nuremberg example, see Roller 1999, figs. 168–71, 182–85, 207–8.

50. Lüdke 1983, p. 131, observes that Hans von Reutlingen of Aachen's signed goldsmith works vary in appearance, since he collaborated with different sculptors.

51. Lüdke 1983, pp. 295–435.

52. Inv. no. DMA 3039. Augsburg 1965, no. 269; Fritz 1982, p. 286; Lüdke 1983, pp. 305–6, no. 5; and Thierbach 2003, no. 16.

53. Abraham Mendlin, the abbey's custodian, commissioned *Saint Christopher*. It bears the arms of Abbot Georg Kastner (r. 1490–1509) and the names of Duke Christoph of Bavaria and Friedrich the Wise, elector of Saxony, who donated funds for its purchase. Augsburg 1965, no. 275.

54. On the secularization, see "The Kimbell Virgin and Child as a Collector's Object" in this volume.

55. Lieb 1947; Augsburg 1965, pp. 196–202, nos. 270–74; Weber 1966, especially pp. 48–68; Fritz 1982, especially pp. 184–85, 286–87; Thierbach 2003, pp. 33–36, nos. 14, 18, 21, 23–24. He also made designs for architecture and sculpture.

56. For a similar monstrance, see Thierbach 2003, no. 17.

57. The altar was evacuated in 1535 because of religious upheaval and again in 1632, before the Swedish occupation of Augsburg. It is last documented in Admont monastery in Austria in 1704, when it was melted down. Russ 2004, pp. 92–93, 102. Krause 2002, fig. 73.

58. Musée Bonnat, Bayonne, inv. no. 1532. Krause 2002, fig. 200.

59. Krause 2002, p. 117. Seld trained Jörg Schweiger, mentioned earlier, and his own brother Nikolaus, who did the 1494 *Ulrich's Cross* for Saints Ulrich and Afra; see Thierbach 2003, no. 20.

60. Lieb 1947, p. 17; Augsburg 1965, no. 270; Fritz 1982, nos. 735–36; Thierbach 2003, no. 18. Krause 2002, pp. 21, 325–26, suggests Holbein designed the exterior scenes.

61. Reindl 1977, p. 188, n. 280.

62. Bernhard was appointed as a canon of Augsburg Cathedral in 1498 and was a candidate for bishop there in 1505 and 1517, as he had been in Eichstätt in 1496. Reindl 1977, pp. 411–12, nos. B 8a–b.

63. Frenzel 1968, pp. 7–11, 13–15, 18; Krause 2002, p. 115, fig. 82.

64. Cranach 1509; Jahn 1972, pp. 456–544; Bellmann, Harksen, and Werner 1979, pp. 257–67.

65. Cranach 1509, Gang no. 7, Reliquiar no. 5; Jahn 1972, p. 526. The statuette included holy fragments—pieces of Mary's hair; breast milk; clothing, including her veil splattered with Christ's blood; fragments of various places, such as the room of the Annunciation and the spots where she died and was assumed into heaven; and even the wax of the candle she held on her deathbed. Made in 1501/2 by Paul Müllner (Möller) of Nuremberg; Bruck 1903, pp. 219–20, 312.

66. Huber 1975, pp. 13–14; Lüdke 1983, no. 36; Fritz 1982, no. 751.

67. On Wilhelm, see the *Pontifikale Gundekarianum* [Eichstätt MS B4], fol. 41–42v, with transcription in Suttner 1867, pp. 19–20; *Ursprung und Herkommen der Bischöfe von Eichstätt von 745–1597* [Eichstätt MS 22], pp. 73–75; *Vita et Arta Episcoporum Eustettensium: Codex Hartmann* [Eichstätt MS 37], fols. 52–53v (dated 1699); Gretser 1734–41, vol. 10, pp. 870–71; Sax 1884, vol. 1, pp. 329–58; Kraft 1956, pp. 77–79 (Bl. 329a–330b); Schmid 1996, pp. 575–76.

68. Kraft 1956, p. 79 ("viro omnium virtutum ornatissimo"). His tomb inscription lauds his wisdom. Mader 1924, p. 100.

69. Buchner 1997, pp. 83–198.

70. Roth 1899; Appel, Braun, and Hofmann 1987, no. D 1.4.

71. Sax 1884, p. 332.

72. Sax 1884, pp. 339–40. This is the forerunner of the Ludwig Maximilians University of Munich.

73. Mader 1924, pp. 408–17; Buchner 1937–38, vol. 1, pp. 238–39; Schmidt 1996, p. 110.

74. Buchner 1937–38, vol. 1, p. 6; Appel et al. 1988, pp. 13–14, 16, 39.

75. On his castles at Hofstetten, Nassenfels, and Pfünz as well as other regional projects, see Mader 1928, pp. 83, 110, 133, 214, 240, 253, 270; Buchner 1937–38, vol. 2, pp. 214, 288; Buchner 1997, pp. 196–98, 245–52.

76. Mader 1924, pp. 35–41. Upper parts were vaulted in 1480.

77. Mader 1924, pp. 120–25; Braun 1986, pp. 8, 26–29.

78. The vault is inscribed "Wilhelmvs Epvs. Eystetten · 1471." The accompanying new west façade was altered in 1716–18. Mader 1924, pp. 52, 54.

79. Buchner 1937–38, vol. 1, pp. 207–8, 210.

80. According to the *Pontifikale Gundekarianum* [Eichstätt MS B4], the residence was constructed at "maximis expensis." It was rebuilt in the eighteenth century. Mader 1924, p. 522.

81. The western wall originally had a sculpted Holy Grave and a door to the chapter room. Mader 1924, pp. 178–219; Braun 1986, pp. 10–11, 32–41; Schmidt 1996, pp. 79–84.

82. Mader 1924, p. 178; Schmidt 1996, p. 65.

83. Braun 1986, p. 10; Schmidt 1996, pp. 115–19, 151, 153, 156; Nussbaum 2000, p. 200.

84. Shelby 1977, pp. 21, 82–83. Hans Holbein the Elder's portrait drawing of Roriczer (c. 1490) is in Berlin (Kupferstichkabinett, KK no. 5008); see Augsburg 1965, no. 78, fig. 82.

85. See note 1. Bauch and Reiter 1987, pp. 78–80, 129–30.

86. *Pontifikale Gundekarianum* [Eichstätt MS B4], fol. 42; Suttner 1867, pp. 19–20, who provided the date 1488; Kraft 1956, p. 79.

87. Steingräber 1961; Merkl 1999, pp. 347–49, no. 43.

88. The rational bears Johann von Eich's arms but was used first by Wilhelm. Mader 1924, pp. 140–41, pl. XIII, and fig. 94 (c. 1750 replacement); Wilckens 1975–76.

89. Mader 1924, pp. 201–2, pl. XXI; Braun 1986, p. 37. The Virgin of the Apocalypse appears earlier on the Mortuarium epitaph of Sigismund von Eyb (d. 1483); Mader 1924, p. 194, fig. 139.

90. I wish to thank Emanuel Braun for sending me this text. The petition derives from Marian litanies, masses, hymns, and common prayers for assistance and forgiveness. Beissel 1909, pp. 62, 302.

91. In 1488 Wilhelm approved a new burgher brotherhood of the Blessed Virgin Mary and Saint Sebastian in Aurach. Perhaps this prompted his inclusion of Sebastian on his own epitaph. Buchner 1937–38, vol. 1, p. 46.

92. The order is, beginning in the east aisle, from north to south, Wilhelm's coat of arms, Virgin and Child of the Apocalypse, two angels blowing the horns of the Last Judgment, John the Baptist, Peter and Paul, Stephen, Sixtus, Sebastian; and in the west aisle, Willibald, Christ as Judge of the World, Richard, Walburga, Wunibald, Bishop Saint, Saint Sola, and a skeleton. Mader 1924, pp. 181, 183; Schmidt 1996, pp. 77–78.

93. Neuhofer 1934, pp. 19–21, 24–27 for Wilhelm's burial services.

94. The stone was quarried in Adnet bei Hallein in the Tyrol. It is signed "Hans Pewrl … von Augsb … hat de. sti. g. m." The main inscription praises Wilhelm's wisdom and his friendship with emperors and kings. The full text is given in Mader 1924, p. 100, pl. X. Beierlein also carved the tomb of Friedrich von Zollern, bishop of Augsburg (r. 1486–1505), now in Augsburg Cathedral. The tombs are very similar in terms of material and basic composition, though Saint Andrew not William introduces Friedrich. Scholars debate which tomb came first, though I suspect that these may have been carved at about the same time. See Halm 1926–27, vol. 1, pp. 102–8, figs. 99, 101–2; Reindl 1977, pp. 95, 196; Chevalley 1995, pp. 293–94, 296.

95. The altar was restored in 1973–75. Mader 1924, pp. 70–72; Buchner 1937–38, vol. 1, p. 207, 210; Braun 1986, pp. 9, 15, 61–65; Grund 1992, pp. 28, 30, nos. 22–32, 109.30–31, 112.4.

96. Warner 1976, p. xvii (quoting Caelius Sedulius).

97. Levi d'Ancona 1957, pp. 3–13, 27; Ringbom 1962, pp. 326–30; Schiller 1980, pp. 154–78; Mayberry 1991, pp. 207–24; Silver forthcoming; Vetter 1958–59, pp. 32–71; and Smeyers 1994, pp. 271–99. I wish to thank Larry Silver for sharing his essay.

98. The full prayer in translation reads: "Hail, Most Holy Mary, Mother of God, Queen of Heaven, Gate of Paradise, Lady of the World, you are the one pure virgin: yourself conceived without sin, you conceived Jesus without any stain. You have borne the Creator and Saviour of the World in whom I do not doubt. Deliver me from every evil and pray for my sin. Amen." Campbell 1998, p. 240.

99. Hollstein 1954–, vols. 24–24a, no. 202.

100. Schiller 1980, pp. 199–204; Winston-Allen 1997.

101. Mader 1924, pp. 188–89, pl. XVIII; Frenzel 1968, pp. 13–15, 18.

102. Mader 1924, p. 188, pl. XVII; Frenzel 1968, pp. 11–13; Braun 1986, p. 38. On the theme, see Beissel 1909, pp. 352–64; Schiller 1980, pp. 195–98. A fragment of a *Virgin of the Apocalypse* (late 1490s) fills another window. Mader 1924, p. 188, fig. 131.

103. Bishop Johann van Eich introduced the Windesheim reforms into the diocese. The influential Augustinian monastery at Rebdorf, just outside of Eichstätt, embraced the reforms and possessed numerous texts by Geert Grote (1340–1384), Thomas à Kempis (1379/80–1471), and other leading writers of this movement, also known as the Modern Devotion. These authors advocated summoning up images of Christ or Mary in their souls. Fink-Lang 1985, pp. 142–49, 183–202; Honée 1994.

104. Wieck 1997, pp. 51–78, here 51, and 138–40 (Hours of the Virgin). Bishop Wilhelm's *Pontifikal-Missale* [Eichstätt MS 131; dated 1466], fols. 143–65 includes the Office of the Virgin and numerous Marian prayers. Mader 1924, pp. 631–35; B. Appel in Kurras and Machilek 1982, no. 29.

105. Wieck 1997, p. 54.

106. Jezler 1994.

107. Buchner 1937–38, vol. 1, p. 6.

108. Jahn 1972, pp. 456–57.

109. Moeller 1971, p. 55.

110. Schlecht 1889; and Mader 1924, pp. 18, 615. Staiger vividly recounts the horrors of these years, including the burning of her own church, which Bishop Wilhelm had consecrated.

111. Mader 1924, pp. 744–48.

112. Sax 1884, pp. 737–65; and Mader 1924, p. 20.

113. Kirmeier and Treml 1991. For an excellent discussion of the impact of the secularization and the subsequent rise in collecting in Cologne, see Kier and Zehnder 1995, especially pp. 77–84.

114. Sax 1884, p. 758.

115. Thierbach 2003, no. 16.

116. Thierbach 2003, no. 18 with provenance.

117. Sheehan 2000, chap. 2 and 3.

118. Glanville 2004, pp. 36–43, is the best source on Mayer Carl.

119. The house is today the Jewish Museum. On its history, see Prévost-Marcilhacy 1995, pp. 50, 303; and www.juedischesmuseum.de/geschichte.

120. Prévost-Marcilhacy 1995, pp. 63, 303–4. In 1891 the property was sold to the city of Frankfurt. The palace was razed to make room for a public park.

121. Pechstein 1974; Nuremberg 1985, no. 15; Glanville 2004, p. 37, who mentions that the asking price was 800,000 guilders, a remarkable sum. After Mayer Carl's wife's death, the German state unsuccessfully tried to buy it.

122. Luthmer 1883–85.

123. I wish to thank Norbert Jopek for sharing with me a rough draft of his article "'Pickert's shop . . . a very labyrinth': Die Kunsthändler Abraham, Siegmund und Max Pickert in Fürth und Nürnberg," which will appear in the *Anzeiger des Germanischen Nationalmuseums*. This is my main source of information on the Pickerts. Also Deneke and Kahsnitz 1978, pp. 711, 731–32, 765–66, 781–82, 791, 808, 812, 816, 839, 1008.

124. *Verzeichniss des Bestandes der Freiherrlich Carl von Rothschild'schen Sammlung auf der Gunthersburg welche im December 1886 zur Vertheilung gelangt ist*, no. 65a. This information was supplied by Nancy E. Edwards (Kimbell Art Museum).

125. Mayer Carl's house, with its three showrooms, was renovated in the 1980s.

126. Her husband was Nathan James Edouard Rothschild (1844–1881). The provenance was supplied by Daniel Katz Ltd., and corrected by Nancy E. Edwards (Kimbell Art Museum). Some of the possessions of Berthe Clara (1862–1903), Mayer Carl's daughter and wife of Alexandre Berthier (1836–1911), prince de Wagram, were sold at the Galerie Georges Petit in Paris on June 12–13, 1911; *Orfèvrerie allemande pierre dures montis provenant de l'ancienne collection de feu M. le Baron Carl Mayer de Rothschild (de Francfort)*.

127. Kohlhaussen 1968, nos. 259, 358, 375, 379, 480.

128. Glanville 2004, p. 40.

Bibliography

Manuscripts

Eichstätt MS B4
Pontifikale Gundekarianum. Eichstätt, Diözesanarchiv Ordinariatsbibliothek. MS Codex B4.

Eichstätt MS 22
Ursprung und Herkommen der Bischöfe von Eichstätt von 745–1597. Eichstätt, Diözesanarchiv Ordinariatsbibliothek. MS 22.

Eichstätt MS 37
Vita et Arta Episcoporum Eustettensium: Codex Hartmann. Eichstätt, Diözesanarchiv Ordinariatsbibliothek. MS 37. Dated 1699.

Eichstätt MS 131
Pontifikal-Missale des Bischofs Wilhelm von Reichenau. Eichstätt, Diözesanarchiv Ordinariatsbibliothek. MS 131. Dated 1466.

Published Works

Aikema and Brown 2000
Bernard Aikema and Beverly Louise Brown, eds. *Renaissance Venice and the North: Crosscurrents in the Time of Bellini, Dürer, and Titian.* New York, 2000.

Appel, Braun, and Hofmann 1987
Brun Appel, Emanuel Braun, and Siegfried Hofmann, eds. *Hl. Willibald, 787–1987: Künder des Glaubens; Pilger, Mönch, Bischof.* Exh. cat. Eichstätt, Diözesan. Eichstätt, 1987.

Appel et al. 1988
Brun Appel et al. *500 Jahre Kloster Marienburg: Beiträge zum Jubiläum der Gründung des Augustinerinnenklosters, 1488.* Abenberg, 1988.

Augsburg 1965
Hans Holbein der Ältere und die Kunst der Spätgotik. Exh. cat. Augsburg, Rathaus. Augsburg, 1965.

Bauch and Reiter 1987
Andreas Bauch and Ernst Reiter, eds. *Das Pontifikale Gundekarianum: Faksimile; Ausgabe des Codex B4 im Diözesanarchiv Eichstätt.* 2 vols. Wiesbaden, 1987.

Beissel 1909
Stephan Beissel. *Geschichte der Verehrung Marias in Deutschland während des Mittelalters.* Freiburg im Breisgau, 1909.

Bellmann, Harksen, and Werner 1979
Fritz Bellmann, Marie-Luise Harksen, and Roland Werner. *Die Denkmale der Lutherstadt Wittenberg.* Weimar, 1979.

80

Bern 1979
Niklaus Manuel Deutsch: Maler, Dichter, Staatsmann. Exh. cat. Bern, Kunstmuseum. Bern, 1979.

Biller 2001
Josef H. Biller. "Beschreibung der Darstellung von Eichstätt aus 'Die Reisebilder Ottheinrichs aus den Jahren 1536/1537.'" *Sammelblatt des Historischen Vereins Eichstätt* 4 (2001), pp. 25–35.

Braun 1986
Emanuel Braun. *Eichstätt: Dom und Domschatz.* Königstein im Taunus, 1986.

Braunfels 1979–89
Wolfgang Braunfels. *Die Kunst im Heiligen Römischen Reich.* 6 vols. Munich, 1979–89.

Buchner 1937–38
Franz Xaver Buchner. *Das Bistum Eichstätt.* 2 vols. Eichstätt, 1937–38.

Buchner 1997
Franz Xaver Buchner. "Kirchliche Zustände in der Diözese Eichstätt am Ausgange des XV. Jahrhunderts" and "Kirchenbauten und Kirchenfabriken in der Eichstätter Diöcese vor 400 Jahren: Bauthatigkeit unter Bischof Wilhelm von Reichenau." In Franz Xaver Buchner. *Klerus, Kirche und Frömmigkeit im spätmittelalterlichen Bistum Eichstätt.* Enno Bünz and Klaus Walter Littger, eds., pp. 83–198 and 245–52. St. Ottilien, 1997.

Bruck 1903
Robert Bruck. *Friedrich der Weise als Förderer der Kunst.* Strasbourg, 1903.

Campbell 1998
Lorne Campbell. *National Gallery Catalogues: The Fifteenth-Century Netherlandish Schools.* London, 1998.

Cherry 1992
John Cherry. *Medieval Craftsmen: Goldsmiths.* London, 1992.

Chevalley 1995
Denis A. Chevalley. *Der Dom zu Augsburg.* Munich, 1995.

Cranach 1509
Lukas Cranach. *Wittenberger Heiltumsbuch: Faksimile-Neudruck der Ausgabe Wittenberg, 1509.* Unterschneidheim, 1969.

Deneke and Kahsnitz 1978
Bernward Deneke and Rainer Kahsnitz, eds. *Das Germanische Nationalmuseum Nürnberg, 1852–1977.* Munich, 1978.

Fink-Lang 1985
Monika Fink-Lang. *Untersuchungen zum Eichstätter Geistesleben im Zeitalter des Humanismus.* Regensburg, 1985.

Frenzel 1968
Gottfried Frenzel. "Die Farbverglasung des Mortuariums im Dom zu Eichstätt." *Anzeiger des Germanischen Nationalmuseums* (1968), pp. 7–26.

Fritz 1982
Johann Michael Fritz. *Goldschmiedekunst der Gotik in Mitteleuropa.* Munich, 1982.

Füssel 2005
Stephan Füssel. *Gutenberg and the Impact of Printing.* Trans. Douglas Martin. Aldershot, 2005.

Geissmar and Louis 1995
Christoph Geissmar and Eleonora Louis, eds. *Glaube, Hoffnung, Liebe, Tod.* Exh. cat. Vienna, Graphische Sammlung Albertina. 2nd ed. Vienna, 1995.

Glanville 2004
Philippa Glanville. "Mayer Carl von Rothschild: Collector or Patriot?" *The Rothschild Archive Review of the Year 2003–2004* (2004), pp. 36–43.

Gretser 1734–41
Jakob Gretser. *Theologi opera omnia.* 17 vols. Regensburg, 1734–41.

Gropp 1999
David Gropp. *Das Ulmer Chorgestühl und Jörg Syrlin der Ältere*. Berlin, 1999.

Grund 1992
Claudia Grund. *Der Dom zu Eichstätt im 19. Jahrhundert: Entwurfzeichnungen, Ansichten*. Wiesbaden, 1992.

Häberle 1934
Adolf Häberle. *Die Goldschmeide zu Ulm*. Ulm, 1934.

Halm 1926–27
Philipp Maria Halm. *Studien zur süddeutschen Plastik*. 2 vols. Augsburg, 1926–27.

Hernad 1990
Béatrice Hernad. *Die Graphiksammlung des Humanisten Hartmann Schedel*. Exh. cat. Munich, Bayerische Staatsbibliothek. Munich, 1990.

Hofmann 1992
Siegfried Hofmann. "Ingolstadt." In *Schätz deutscher Goldschmiedekunst von 1500 bis 1920 aus dem Germanischen Nationalmuseum,* ed. Klaus Pechstein et al. Exh. cat. Ingolstadt, Stadtmuseum. Berlin, 1992, pp. 113–16.

Hollstein 1954–
Friedrich W. H. Hollstein, ed. *German Engravings, Etchings, and Woodcuts, ca. 1400–1700*. Vols. 1–. Amsterdam, 1954–. Vols. 24–24a (1986), ed. Fritz Koreny.

Honée 1994
Eugène Honée. "Image and Imagination in the Medieval Culture of Prayer: A Historical Perspective." In Henk van Os, ed. *The Art of Devotion in the Late Middle Ages in Europe, 1300–1500*. Exh. cat. Amsterdam, Rijksmuseum. Princeton, 1994, pp. 157–74.

Huber 1975
Josef Huber. *Pfarr- und Wallfahrtskirche Kösslarn*. Munich, 1975. 1st ed., 1964.

Huth 1967
Hans Huth. *Künstler und Werkstatt der Spätgotik*. Darmstadt, 1967.

Jahn 1972
Johannes Jahn, intro. *Lucas Cranach d. Ä., 1472–1553: Das gesamte graphische Werk*. Munich, 1972.

Jezler 1994
Peter Jezler, ed. *Himmel, Hölle, Fegefeuer: Das Jenseits im Mittelalter*. Exh. cat. Zürich, Schweizerisches Landesmuseum. Munich, 1994.

Jopek 2002
Norbert Jopek. *German Sculpture, 1430–1540: A Catalogue of the Collection in the Victoria and Albert Museum*. London, 2002.

Kier and Zehnder 1995
Hiltrud Kier and Frank Günter Zehnder. *Lust und Verlust: Kölner Sammler zwischen Trikolore und Preussenadler*. Cologne, 1995.

Kirmeier and Treml 1991
Josef Kirmeier and Manfred Treml, eds. *Glanz und Ende der alten Klöster: Säkularisation im bayerischen Oberland, 1803*. Exh. cat. Kloster Benediktbeuren. Munich, 1991.

Kirschbaum and Braunfels 1968–76
Engelbert Kirschbaum and Wolfgang Braunfels, eds. *Lexikon der christliche Ikonographie*. 8 vols. Rome, 1968–76.

Kohlhaussen 1968
Heinrich Kohlhaussen. *Nürnberger Goldschmiedekunst des Mittelalters und der Dürerzeit, 1240 bis 1540*. Berlin, 1968.

Kraft 1956
Wilhelm Kraft. *Die Eichstätter Bischofschronik der Grafen Wilhelm Werner von Zimmern*. Würzburg, 1956.

Krause 2002
Katharina Krause. *Hans Holbein der Ältere*. Munich, 2002.

Kurras and Machilek 1982
Lotte Kurras and Franz Machilek, eds. *Caritas Pirckheimer, 1467–1532*. Exh. cat. Nuremberg, Kaiserburg. Munich, 1982.

82

Landau and Parshall 1994
David Landau and Peter Parshall. *The Renaissance Print, 1470–1550.* New Haven, 1994.

Levi d'Ancona 1957
Mirella Levi d'Ancona. *The Iconography of the Immaculate Conception in the Middle Ages and the Early Renaissance.* New York, 1957.

Lieb 1947
Norbert Lieb. *Jörg Seld: Goldschmied und Bürger von Augsburg.* Munich, 1947.

Lightbown 1989
Ronald Lightbown. *Sandro Botticelli: Life and Work.* New York, 1989.

Lüdke 1983
Dietmar Lüdke. *Die Statuetten der gotischen Goldschmiede.* 2 vols. Munich, 1983.

Luthmer 1883–85
Ferdinand Luthmer. *Der Schatz Carl von Rothschild.* 2 vols. Frankfurt, 1883–85.

Luthmer 1890
Ferdinand Luthmer, ed. *Führer durch die Freiherrlich K. von Rothschild'sche Kunstsammlung.* Frankfurt am Main, 1890.

Mader 1924
Felix Mader. *Die Kunstdenkmäler von Mittelfranken.* Vol. 1, *Stadt Eichstätt.* Munich, 1924. Reprint, 1981.

Mader 1928
Felix Mader. *Die Kunstdenkmäler von Mittelfranken.* Vol. 2, *Bezirksamt Eichstätt.* Munich, 1928. Reprint, 1982.

Marsch, Biller, and Jacob 2001
Angelika Marsch, Josef H. Biller, and Frank-Dietrich Jacob, eds. *Die Reisebilder Pfalzgraf Ottheinrichs aus den Jahren 1536/37.* 2 vols. Weissenhorn, 2001.

Mayberry 1991
Nancy Mayberry. "The Controversy over the Immaculate Conception in Medieval and Renaissance Art, Literature, and Society." *Journal of Medieval and Renaissance Studies* 21 (1991), pp. 207–24.

Meininghaus 2000
Heiner Meininghaus. "Eichstätt Goldschmiedemarken: Neue Forschungsergebnisse, Teil 35." *Weltkunst* 70 (June 2000), pp. 1076–78.

Merkl 1999
Ulrich Merkl. *Buchmalerei in Bayern in der ersten Hälfte des 16. Jahrhunderts.* Regensburg, 1999.

Moeller 1971
Bernd Moeller. "Piety in Germany around 1500." In *The Reformation in Medieval Perspective*, Steven Ozment, ed., pp. 50–75. Chicago, 1971.

Neuhofer 1934
Theodor Neuhofer. *Gabriel von Eyb: Fürstbischof von Eichstätt, 1455–1535.* Eichstätt, 1934.

Neuhofer 1971
Theodor Neuhofer. "Die älteren Pirckheimer und Eichstätt." *Sammelblatt des Historischen Vereins Eichstätt* 64 (1971), pp. 85–92.

Nuremberg 1985
Wenzel Jamnitzer und die Nürnberger Goldschmiedekunst, 1500–1700. Exh. cat. Nuremberg, Germanisches Nationalmuseum. Munich, 1985.

New York and Nuremberg 1986
Gothic and Renaissance Art in Nuremberg, 1300–1550. Exh. cat. New York, Metropolitan Museum of Art, and Nuremberg, Germanisches Nationalmuseum. Munich, 1986.

Nussbaum 2000
Norbert Nussbaum. *German Gothic Church Architecture.* Trans. Scott Kleager. New Haven, 2000.

Nuttall 2004

Paula Nuttall. *From Flanders to Florence: The Impact of Netherlandish Painting, 1400–1500.* New Haven, 2004.

Van Os et al. 2000

Henk van Os et al. *The Way to Heaven: Relic Veneration in the Middle Ages.* Baarn, 2000.

Pechstein 1974

Klaus Pechstein. "Der Merkelsche Tafelaufsatz von Wenzel Jamnitzer." *Mitteilungen des Vereins für Geschichte der Stadt Nürnberg* 61 (1974), pp. 90–121.

Potts 2003

Timothy Potts, ed. *Kimbell Art Museum: Handbook of the Collection.* New Haven, 2003.

Prévost-Marcilhacy 1995

Pauline Prévost-Marcilhacy. *Les Rothschild: bâtisseurs et mécènes.* Paris, 1995.

Reindl 1977

Peter Reindl. *Loy Hering.* Basel, 1977.

Ringbom 1962

Sixten Ringbom. "Maria in Sole and the Virgin of the Rosary." *Journal of the Courtauld and Warburg Institutes* 25 (1962), pp. 326–30.

Roller 1999

Stefan Roller. *Nürnberger Bildhauerkunst der Spätgotik.* Munich, 1999.

Rosenberg 1922–25

Marc Rosenberg. *Der goldschmiede Merkzeichen.* 4 vols. Frankfurt, 1922–25.

Roth 1899

F. W. E. Roth. "Michael Reyser, 1478–1494." *Sammelblatt des Historischen Vereins Eichstätt* 14 (1899), pp. 1–40.

Rowlands with Bartrum 1993

John Rowlands with Giulia Bartrum. *Drawings by German Artists in the Department of Prints and Drawings in the British Museum: The Fifteenth Century, and the Sixteenth Century by Artists born before 1530.* 2 vols. London, 1993.

Russ 2004

Sabine Russ. *Gabriel Dreer (um 1580–1631) und die Kunsttätigkeit der Klöster Admont und Ottobeuren.* Ed. Matthias Kunze. Munich, 2004.

Sauter 2001

Martin Sauter. "Beobachtungen zu Technik und Oberflächenbearbeitung von Goldschmiedearbeiten." In *Das Basler Münsterschatz,* pp. 286–92. Exh. cat. Basel, Historisches Museum. Basel, 2001.

Sax 1884

Julius Sax. *Die Bischöfe und Reichsfürsten von Eichstädt, 745–1806.* 2 vols. Landshut, 1884.

Schiller 1980

Gertrud Schiller. *Ikonographie der christlichen Kunst.* Vol. 4.2, *Maria.* Gütersloh, 1980.

Schlecht 1889

Joseph Schlecht, ed. *Eichstätt im Swedenkriege: Tagebuch der Augustinernonne Clara Staiger, Priorin des Klosters Mariastein, über die Kriegjahre 1631 bis 1650.* Eichstätt, 1889.

Schmid 1996

Alois Schmid. "Reichenau, Wilhelm von." In *Die Bischöfe des Heiligen Römischen Reiches, 1448 bis 1648: Ein biographisches Lexikon,* Erwin Gatz, ed., pp. 575–76. Berlin, 1996.

Schmidt 1996

Michael Schmidt. *Das Mortuarium am Eichstätter Dom: Eine architekturhistorische Untersuchung.* Eichstätt, 1996.

Schoch, Mende, and Scherbaum 2002
Rainer Schoch, Matthias Mende, and Anna Scherbaum, eds. *Albrecht Dürer: Das druckgraphische Werk.* Vol. 2, *Holzschnitte und Holzschnittfolgen.* Munich, 2002.

Schwemmer 1973
Wilhelm Schwemmer. "Freiheit und Organisationszwang der Nürnberg Maler in reichsstädtischer Zeit." *Mitteilungen des Vereins für Geschichte der Stadt Nürnberg* 60 (1973), pp. 222–49.

Seling 1980
Helmut Seling. *Die Kunst der Augsburger Goldschmiede, 1529–1868.* 3 vols. Munich, 1980.

Sheehan 2000
James J. Sheehan. *Museums in the German Art World from the End of the Old Regime to the Rise of Modernism.* Oxford, 2000.

Shelby 1977
Lon R. Shelby, ed. *Gothic Design Techniques: The Fifteenth-Century Design Booklets of Mathes Roriczer and Hanns Schmuttermayer.* London, 1977.

Silver forthcoming
Larry Silver. "Full of Grace: 'Mariolatry' in Post-Reformation Germany." In *The Idol in the Era of Art*, Michael Cole and Rebecca Zorach, eds. Aldershot, forthcoming.

Smeyers 1994
Maurits Smeyers. "Het Marianum of Onze-Lieve-Vrouw-in-de-zon: Getuige van een laat-middeleeuwse devotie." *Nederlands Kunsthistorisch Jaarboek* 45 (1994), pp. 271–99.

Smith 1983
Jeffrey Chipps Smith. *Nuremberg: A Renaissance City, 1500–1618.* Exh. cat. Austin, Archer M. Huntington Art Gallery, University of Texas. Austin, 1983.

Smith 2004
Jeffrey Chipps Smith. *The Northern Renaissance.* London, 2004.

Steinberg 1996
Leo Steinberg. *The Sexuality of Christ in Renaissance Art and in Modern Oblivion.* 2nd ed. Chicago, 1996.

Steingräber 1961
Erich Steingräber. "Beiträge zum Werk des Augsburger Buchmalers Ulrich Taler." *Pantheon* 19 (1961), pp. 119–26.

Suttner 1867
Joseph Georg Suttner. *Tabula Leonrodiana Eystettensis explicata & illustrat: Accedunt vitae Pontificum Eystettensium ad saeculum usque XVI ex pontificali Gundecariano descriptae.* Eichstätt, 1867. [*Pastoral-Blatt des Bisthums Eichstätt* 14 (1867).]

Tanner 1991
Paul Tanner. *Das Amerbach-Kabinett: Die Basler Goldschmiederisse.* Exh. cat. Basel, Kupferstichkabinett der Öffentlichen Kunstsammlung. Basel, 1991.

Thierbach 2003
Melanie Thierbach, ed. *Gold und Silber: Augsburgs glänzende Exportwaren.* Exh. cat Augsburg, Diözesanmuseum St. Afra. Augsburg, 2003.

Ulm 2002
Michel Erhart & Jörg Syrlin d. Ä.: Spätgotik in Ulm. Exh. cat. Ulmer Museum. Stuttgart, 2002.

Vetter 1958–59
Ewald M. Vetter. "Mulier amicta sole und Mater Salvatoris." *Münchner Jahrbuch der bildenden Kunst*, 3rd ser., 9–10 (1958–59), pp. 32–71.

Warner 1976
Marina Warner. *Alone of All Her Sex: The Myth and the Cult of the Virgin Mary.* New York, 1976.

Weber 1966
Ingrid Weber. "Die Tiefenbronner Monstranz und ihr künstlerischer Umkreis." *Anzeiger des Germanischen Nationalmuseums* (1966), pp. 7–87.

Wieck 1997
Roger S. Wieck. *Painted Prayers: The Book of Hours in Medieval and Renaissance Art*. Exh. cat. New York, Pierpont Morgan Library. New York, 1997.

Wilckens 1975–76
Leonie von Wilckens. "Das Rationale des Eichstätter Bischofs Johann von Eich (1445–64)." *Jahrbuch der bayerischen Denkmalpflege* 30 (1975–76), pp. 119–28.

Wilson 1976
Adrian Wilson. *The Making of the Nuremberg Chronicle*. Amsterdam, 1976.

Winston-Allen 1997
Anne Winston-Allen. *Stories of the Rose: The Making of the Rosary in the Middle Ages*. University Park, Pa., 1997.

Photograph Credits

The *Kimbell Virgin and Child* was photographed by Robert LaPrelle.

Most of the photographs of works of art were provided by the owners.
Others were supplied courtesy of the following institutions and individuals:
Photographed by Helmut Bauer (fig. 68)
Photograph © 2006 Museum of Fine Arts, Boston (fig. 26)
© Copyright the Trustees of the British Museum (fig. 35)
© Institut für Realienkunde des Mittelalters und der frühen Neuzeit. Photographed by Peter Böttcher (fig. 66)
Photo: Friedrich 1964 (fig. 49)
© Kunstmuseum Basel (figs. 33, 34)
Photographed by Ingeborg Limmer (figs. 60, 61, 62, 69, 71, 72)
© Réunion des Musées Nationaux/Art Resource, NY. Photographed by G. Blot (fig. 47)
Copyright © Rijksmuseum Amsterdam (fig. 77)
Scala/Art Resource, NY (figs. 27, 29)
Photograph courtesy of Kenneth Thomson and the Art Gallery of Ontario, Toronto (fig. 52)
© V&A Picture Library (fig. 36)
© Copyright 2003 Wittelsbacher Ausgleichsfonds München (fig. 53)
Photographed by Horst Ziegenfusz (fig. 76)